WIT
D0589097

Choice and the End of Social Housing

National Assembly for Wales Library

5004001953287

WITHDRAWN

Choice and the End of Social Housing

PETER KING

The Institute of Economic Affairs

First published in Great Britain in 2006 by
The Institute of Economic Affairs
2 Lord North Street
Westminster
London SW1P 3LB
in association with Profile Books Ltd

The mission of the Institute of Economic Affairs is to improve public understanding of the fundamental institutions of a free society, with particular reference to the role of markets in solving economic and social problems.

Copyright © The Institute of Economic Affairs 2006

The moral right of the authors has been asserted.

All rights reserved. Without limiting the rights under copyright reserved above, no part of this publication may be reproduced, stored or introduced into a retrieval system, or transmitted, in any form or by any means (electronic, mechanical, photocopying, recording or otherwise), without the prior written permission of both the copyright owner and the publisher of this book.

A CIP catalogue record for this book is available from the British Library.

ISBN 978 0 255 36568 0

Many IEA publications are translated into languages other than English or are reprinted. Permission to translate or to reprint should be sought from the Director General at the address above.

Typeset in Stone by MacGuru Ltd
info@macguru.org.uk

CONTENTS

THE AUTHOR

Peter King is Reader in Social Thought at the Centre for Comparative Housing Research, De Montfort University, Leicester. He is considered a pioneer in the area of the social philosophy of housing, researching on the relationship of housing to key concepts such as rights, needs and equality. He has also written on the issues of privacy and the meaning and use of housing. He is the author of eight books including *Housing, Individuals and the State* (Routledge, 1998) and *A Social Philosophy of Housing* (Ashgate, 2003), as well as the textbook *Understanding Housing Finance* (Routledge, 2001). In 2004 he contributed a chapter to the IEA publication *Economy and Virtue*, and also wrote a paper on housing benefit for the Adam Smith Institute in 2000. His most recent book is entitled *A Conservative Consensus?: Housing Policy before 1997 and After* (Imprint Academic, 2006). Like most academics working on housing issues, Peter is an owner-occupier, but he has been a housing association tenant and was brought up in council and tied accommodation.

FOREWORD

Almost every aspect of housing policy in the UK is dominated by central planning and socialist methods of resource allocation. Central governments determine how many houses should be built. Local government imposes constraints on the way in which houses can be constructed and where they can be built. Building regulations stifle innovation and impose standards, regardless of the preferences of those who will ultimately own a property. As in so many other areas of economic life, however, it is the poor who suffer most from state control. A whole language has been developed to obscure the genuine nature of state intervention in housing for the poor. A specified percentage of new houses on particular sites is generally designated 'social housing', as if the other houses are somehow not 'social' or are 'anti-social'. A certain number of houses have to be 'affordable', as if any builder would ever build a house that was not affordable. Social housing is a euphemism for housing controlled by political authority. Affordable housing is a euphemism for subsidised housing – although the source of the subsidies is often incredibly opaque.

It is the poor who lose most from this state control of their housing. Replacing systems of controls, state planning and opaque subsidies with straightforward income transfers to the poor can result in massive welfare gains. While there have been market-oriented innovations in policy in the last 30 years, such as 'Right to Buy' and the introduction of some liberalisation to private renting, since 1988 policy has become increasingly dominated by the assumption that government organisation and control are necessary to provide better housing for the poor. Since the 1990s such policy has been dressed up in the language of choice. Yet, as Peter King explains in this monograph, the true nature of housing policy is that it is becoming more and more centralised and controlled by the state.

After discussing the merits of different approaches to housing policy and analysing current policy, Peter King makes proposals for change. He proposes a straightforward subsidy, based on income, to meet housing needs, with some advisory support to those who may, for various reasons, be unable to make effective choices in the market. His proposals would be a logical extension of some of the policies followed in the 1980s. In particular, it would be a logical extension of the Right-to-Buy policy brought in by the first Thatcher government. Providing income subsidies to help people pay market-based rents, to live in houses provided either by housing associations or private landlords, would empower and provide choice to the very people the provision of so-called 'social housing' is meant to help. Simultaneously, it would remove many distortions in the housing market and help nurture innovation in the provision of rented housing.

By the author's own admission, there are certain risks with the proposed reforms. It could be argued that they do not go far enough. The objectives of reform would also be helped if there were wider-ranging reform of the whole social security system. Nevertheless, Peter King does provide a compelling argument that promoting choice and provision of so-called social housing are incompatible and that, if we have to choose between the two policies, then promoting choice is the better approach.

As in all IEA publications, the views expressed in Hobart Paper 155 are those of the author and not those of the Institute (which has no corporate view), its managing trustees, Academic Advisory Council members or senior staff.

PHILIP BOOTH

Editorial and Programme Director,
Institute of Economic Affairs
Professor of Insurance and Risk Management,
Sir John Cass Business School, City University
June 2006

SUMMARY

- Housing is particularly amenable to policies that promote choice because housing needs are predictable and housing is a relatively simple product to understand.
- Although there was some movement in the 1980s towards housing subsidies being given to individuals, rather than to developers or landlords, the provision of social housing in the UK is still centrally controlled and subsidised. Countries such as Australia and New Zealand and some European countries have successfully adopted policies of subsidising only tenants.
- Subsidising tenants not only promotes choice, it also removes stigma from social housing, allows more effective targeting and prevents producer capture of housing policy.
- Current government policy purports to promote choice and 'put people first', whereas, in reality, the genuine control that tenants have over their choice of dwelling has been reduced. Furthermore, both rents and quality of housing are being increasingly controlled by central government.
- Private finance and stock transfer have not given greater choice to tenants nor reduced local or central government control of housing. Also, local government is being increasingly controlled by central government: in King's words, 'the government is always there to tell housing

organisations what they should do with their autonomy'.

- Housing policy is being deliberately obscured by incomprehensible language. Concepts such as 'Supporting People', the 'Decent Homes Standard' and the 'Together We Can' initiative are empty of meaning. A rational debate about policy would be better served by using clear language.
- In the future, housing support for those in need should be provided by a straightforward means-tested subsidy that varies only with local rent levels and according to whether the recipient is a single person or part of a couple or a family with children.
- Such a system of subsidies should be financed by money currently spent on the current housing benefit system and by money spent on subsidies currently given to social housing providers.
- The subsidy would ensure that there was competition between landlords, as no landlord would receive any state support: social housing would come to an end. Tenants would also be supported with advisory services in the early stages of reform.
- The reform of housing policy would be more effective if implemented along with a more wide-ranging review of social security. In the long term it may be desirable to phase out specific subsidies to individuals for housing and replace them with cash social security benefits.

TABLES AND BOXES

PREFACE

Social housing is currently undergoing a period of considerable change, and while this may be seen as an opportunity, it also
poses a significant challenge to the very ethos of social housing,
such that the very nature and purpose of the sector are being
questioned. Moreover, this debate is taking place both within and
outside the sector, among representative bodies of social landlords and housing professionals, and government.

In early 2005 the Office of the Deputy Prime Minster (ODPM)[1]
produced a five-year strategy for housing entitled *Homes for
All* (ODPM, 2005a). What is interesting about this policy is the
manner in which it seemed to signal a change in the focus of
government policy. Instead of concentrating on social housing,
the needs of vulnerable tenants or the homeless, the focus was
on the government's determination to extend owner occupation.
The strategy seems to see 'home' as something that occupiers own
rather than rent. What the government seems to be concerned
with is not the vulnerable or those who cannot gain access to
decent housing, but rather the ability of those on middle incomes,
mainly employed in the public sector, to gain access to owner
occupation in high-cost areas. The housing crisis is seen in terms
of the problem of potential first-time buyers in the South finding it

[1]   The ODPM was renamed the Department of Communities and Local Government (DCLG) in May 2006.

hard to get on the housing ladder. As a result we are seeing a shift in housing policy away from the worst off to support for owner occupation through the development of equity share schemes, key worker schemes and the use of government funding to subsidise new private house building (the so-called £60,000 house). From the government's point of view at least, the housing crisis is therefore not in what is often described as social housing. Indeed, as the government stated in the 2000 Housing Green Paper, 'most people are well housed' (DETR, 2000: 5), and this implies, if not complacency, that there are issues only at the margins which need to be dealt with. This does not mean that there are no problems, but rather it indicates how social housing is actually perceived by the current government: owner occupation is seen as the norm – the aspirational tenure – and hence that is where the priorities lie, even if this means that social housing has to be used to pursue them.

This policy development poses two questions: first, what does it say about the future for social housing? Does it indicate that there is no future, and so might not *Homes for All* signal the end of social housing? But second, and more generally, what does this tell us about the role of government in housing? This monograph answers these two questions, but I want to make some preliminary comments on the second question, as this points directly to a key theme I wish to develop straight away.

What I believe this new and emerging policy shows is that central government is able to control the policy agenda and need not heed housing professionals and commentators. Indeed, it is my contention that many of the policies over the last twenty years have been developed to suit the imperatives of central government at the expense of tenants, applicants and local providers. Policies demanding the use of private finance and the transfer of council housing to housing associations allow the government to achieve its objectives without the full cost falling on the Treasury. The key to understanding recent policy initiatives is that government is able to maintain control even when it no longer provides most of the money. Hence if the affordability of owner-occupied housing is the most pressing political problem, the government feels able to prioritise this over and above the needs and requirements of social housing.

Housing, I shall suggest, is heavily centralised, yet it is one area of welfare that is particularly amenable to choice and individual decision-making. The government appears to appreciate this, as choice has certainly been a key feature of its policy-making in recent years. But I want to question just how far policy is actually meant to enhance choice and how much the idea of choice is just another element in government rhetoric. Indeed, housing has found itself particularly prone to hyperbole and abstractions, seemingly as a means of giving the impression of innovation even when the main element of government policies since 1997 is their continuity with the Thatcherite heritage (King, 2006).

The aim of this monograph is threefold: first, to consider the manner in which social housing has been subsidised and how this has changed and is changing because of current policies; second, to undertake a critique of the current state of housing policy; and, third, to offer proposals for reform. As well as discussing housing subsidies in economic and political terms, I also undertake what might be called a cultural critique of contemporary housing policy, which concentrates on the nature of policy and the manner in which the language of housing policy has changed in recent years. I shall suggest that this is not merely a matter of semantics, but relates to the manner in which social housing is viewed by government. It is my argument that the current government has concerned itself as much with rhetoric as with new thinking, such that, rather than there being new ideas and policies introduced, what we have seen is a continuation of the policies of the 1980s and 1990s but, as it were, 'in new bottles'. We need to appreciate this attempt to redescribe old policies as 'new' and 'innovative' if we are to get the measure of current attitudes towards housing. The concentration on language in this monograph is therefore not gratuitous or marginal to the argument, but rather crucial to understanding how policy is sustained.

This monograph, therefore, is a critique of current government policy and how we might create a more rational alternative based on individual choice. One possible, principled route that one might have taken in criticising current policies would have been to argue against *all and any* government intervention in housing. Indeed, I have developed this form of critique myself in several of my earlier writings on housing (King, 1998, 2003). My aim in this paper, however, is somewhat different. While we might wish that we could start from somewhere other than where we are, we are in fact circumscribed by existing structures, policies and expectations. We might ignore these and state that housing can be provided entirely through markets without any government intervention. But even if this is where we wish to end up, we must be realistic enough to appreciate that we can get there only by using the very structures we criticise and by altering them as expectations change. So here I take on current policy on its own terms and ask whether hard analysis leads us to the conclusion that the government is using the best mechanism to achieve its own objectives.

Therefore much of this monograph is concerned with what is wrong with current policies and how we can move from where we are to where we wish to be. The basis of my critique is that choice is merely used as an attempt to increase supply-side efficiency and transfer risk away from the Treasury and has nothing really to do with individual empowerment. My proposals are aimed at creating real choice through a system based on competition between landlords, and subsidies going directly to the households that need them. But in order to achieve this level of choice it will be necessary to bring social housing to an end: put another way, *choice and social housing just do not mix.*

Choice and the End of Social Housing

1 PUTTING SOCIAL HOUSING IN ITS PLACE

Interesting times

The government has laid out its plans for housing with the 2000 Housing Green Paper, the *Sustainable Communities* plan, published in 2003, and the five-year strategy *Homes for All*, published in 2005. While these changes involve an increase in expenditure on social housing, there is also a heightened emphasis on choice. The specific mechanisms to be introduced involve an enhanced use of stock transfer to lever in private finance, the regulation of rent levels, the reform of housing allowances and an increase in support for owner occupation. These measures involve an apparent increase in commercial disciplines to enhance efficiency, but also a greater level of central regulation, so that all social housing has to meet a common standard of amenity by 2010 and submit to a national rent-setting formula that effectively determines the income of social landlords. One result of this standardisation through centralisation is that social housing has effectively been turned from a local to a national service, with central government assuming the role of planning for its use, financing and improvement.

This heightened centralisation is the context in which we have to view the government's promotion of choice in such areas as the letting of social housing and in the housing benefit system. The government sees no contradiction in these policies. Indeed, this choice agenda has been used to justify centralisation, for example the national rent-setting policy, which seeks to achieve convergence between housing associations and local authorities and thus, it is argued, allow applicants to make choices based on quality of provision and management without regard to affordability. The view from government is that choice can and should be imposed and this will be for the benefit of tenants and taxpayers alike. The belief is that the desired ends matter more than the means, regardless of the fact that the chosen means – central direction of resources and national target-setting – run counter to the notions of autonomy, diversity and individualised decision-making.

But the government is not totally oblivious of the need for diversity in policy-making. It has accepted that differential demand across the country is a problem that needs tackling with flexible policies. In particular, there is a shortage of both afford-able housing for sale and rented housing in the South and East, while there is apparently unwanted social housing in parts of the North. Hence the *Sustainable Communities* plan (ODPM, 2003) proposed new development in growth areas in the South and around London, along with the demolition of housing in other regions. Subsequent to this the *Homes for All* strategy (ODPM, 2005a) aimed to move resources towards low-cost home owner-ship, with preference being given to key public sector workers such as nurses and teachers. The government's view is that those on low incomes should also benefit from owner occupation as the majority currently do. This can be seen as something of a novel development: instead of owner occupation being promoted on the basis of personal responsibility and independence as in the Thatcher years (DOE, 1987), it is now being promoted on social justice grounds. More prosaically, however, one can also see it as arising from the same populist roots as the Right to Buy policy of the early 1980s. Equally significantly, it is similar to Right to Buy in that the policy involves the transfer of public resources into owner occupation with the consequent diminution of resources for social housing. What the *Homes for All* strategy makes explicit, in a manner that the Conservative governments of the 1980s never did, is that social housing is to be subsidiary to the majority tenure and, where necessary, used as a means to further owner occupation. As Clapham (2005) has pointed out, housing policy has shifted away from assisting the poorest to managing demand and access consonant with differential labour market pressures in the north and south of the country.

But there is a sting in the tail here. The *Homes for All* strategy introduces means testing into owner occupation by establishing a system of targeted subsidies to certain 'deserving' households. So again, we see something of a contradiction, in that owner occupation – which offers households choice and personal responsibility – is to be opened up to low-income households by centralised targets and standards.

There is, then, something of a pattern here, of changes aimed at enhancing choice and opportunity, but which are all top-down and initiated by government. What this suggests is that reform is very much controlled and tailored to meet a particular agenda. The government is not seeking a proper liberalisation of housing, whereby it steps back from the controls and allows things to develop in a natural or organic manner. This suggests both that the changes have a purpose, and also that they might not be as comprehensive as the government claims. In particular, there has been no real attempt to alter some of the fundamentals of social housing, such as access on the basis of need; the rigidities between tenures, which impact on subsidies; and funding based on central-ised priorities with new development undertaken through housing associations rather than local authorities. Instead we have seen new policies and practices overlaying these fundamentals, which have been in place since the 1980s. The situation facing social landlords is therefore one of increased complexity within a heavily constrained policy framework largely geared to meet the priorities of central government.

This sense of increasing complexity within a constrained envir-onment has fed the debate on the future direction and purpose of social housing. The prospect and actual effects of stock transfer and increased choice, along with the shift in resources towards owner occupation, have called into question the very future of social housing. If the government is so clearly favouring owner occupation to the extent of using social justice arguments to support its position, then just where is the social housing sector going? Does, and indeed should, the sector still fulfil the same purpose as it has traditionally done? In particular, if social housing is seen as a last resort and owner occupation is now so definitely the tenure of choice, does social housing really have any future?

A question of image?

These questions have increasingly come to the fore as New Labour housing policy has become clear. The sector has tried to answer them. One interesting example was the attempt by the National Housing Federation (NHF), the lobby group for English housing associations, to 'rebrand' social housing. In response to survey evidence that suggested that social housing was for 'losers' and that working in the sector was not seen to be of high status, the NHF employed branding consultants to try to remodel the image of housing associations as being 'iN [*sic*] business for neighbourhoods' (NHF, 2003). The clear aim here was to assert a new identity for social housing providers in the face of structural, political and ideological obstacles. Social housing was seen, rightly or wrongly, to be failing, so the NHF suggested its role should appear to change. The key conclusion of the NHF's 'rebranding' exercise was to assert the extensive range of activities that social landlords were involved in. They were not just landlords, but were, and should be, involved in creating and developing communities, in building diversity and other rather grandiose abstractions. The picture created by the NHF's campaign was that social landlords were involved in a whole gamut of community development, education and employment activities beyond and above their basic activities of housing: it was as if housing, of itself, was not enough for them, and that they were actually embarrassed that their role might be limited *only* to managing and maintaining dwellings for other people to live in. The 'rebranding' exercise sought to extend the role of social landlords and to show just what social landlords can and do achieve.

The whole exercise was somewhat controversial, not only for its apparent acceptance of the view that social housing was failing and housed 'failures', but also for its cost, which was reputed to include consultants' fees in excess of £750,000.[1] What is most significant about this whole exercise is not that it changed the

---

1   There is, of course, something of an irony here, that a body can afford to spend such huge sums to deal with the notion of failure. The apparent situation whereby social landlords can be both failing and asset- and cash-rich was not seen as odd by those involved in the 'rebranding'.

perception of social landlords, but rather just how internalised the process was. It was interesting that the main focus of the 'rebranding' campaign when it was launched in 2003 was to get housing associations – which had paid for the exercise through a compulsory members' levy – to sign up to the campaign themselves and advertise it locally. Thus we had the outcome whereby the perception of social housing was to be changed by the outreach work of the very bodies perceived as the problem.

The key fault of the NHF's campaign was the belief that the sector could be reformed internally; that the image of social housing was dependent on social housing organisations themselves, and not the views of the 80 per cent who do not enjoy it and who would not be seen dead near it. The NHF could not, or would not, appreciate that the image of social housing was due to how it was viewed by people outside the sector looking in and not liking what they saw. In short, the image of the sector could not be altered through internal action. A more realistic prescription of social housing's plight was identified by Tom Manion, the controversial director of Irwell Valley Housing Association, who was quoted in *Inside Housing* (4 March 2005, p. 2) as saying that the 'survival of the sector really depends on how it is still viewed as some sort of welfare stateism with crap customer service'. According to Manion, what matters is making the sector respectable in the eyes of those people who do not live in it, but who effectively pay for it. In his view it is not the landlords or the residents of social housing who are crucial to its survival, but rather the majority who look at it from the outside, who form and make public opinion, who vote, pay taxes, read newspapers, and who compare what they know about social housing with the owner occupation they enjoy. The survival of the social housing sector, therefore, does not depend on any internal repositioning of the role of social landlords, but on how it is perceived externally.

There is, however, a further element to the NHF's reasoning that I want to raise here as a pointer to my later discussion on policy. The key conclusion of the 'rebranding' was that the main role of social landlords was to work to develop and change communities, rather than to manage and maintain their own housing stock. This is a view that has become common in recent years, particularly since the ODPM's *Sustainable Communities* plan (ODPM, 2003) put great stress on the point that community development 'is more than housing' and that it was about the creation of a much wider infrastructure. This is doubtless the case, and the OPDM is certainly right to criticise past housing development for being built in isolation. But, we need to ask, why is it that social landlords extrapolate from this that their main role – their distinguishing feature – is community development and not managing houses? I would suggest that this again relates back to the internal nature of the debate, which focused on the aspirations of the sector rather than how it was actually perceived. This is one aspect of the trend over the last decade or so for housing organisations and commentators to extend the role of social landlords beyond their core functions and involve them in strategic partnerships and community development, instead of encouraging them to concentrate on their core activities where they can legitimately claim expertise.

What this suggests is that social landlords are unsure of their role. If they accept the prevailing view that housing is not enough, the role of social landlords appears to be diminished. It is perhaps natural therefore to seek to become involved in those wider activities identified in the *Sustainable Communities* plan and to diversify.[2] When this is allied to the changes being pushed through by government, which, as we shall see in Chapter 5, are predominantly geared to changing structures, we can see why social landlords might be looking at their role with some trepidation. What is by no means clear, however, is whether they have any real idea about how to deal with their situation.

---

2   One could be really cynical and suggest it was not a coincidence that the NHF began pushing the role of social landlords as community builders just when the government started to wrap its housing and planning policies in the jargon of 'sustainable communities'.

2 HOUSING IS DIFFERENT

What complicates the analysis further is that social housing has a different, and lower, status within the welfare state than other government-provided services. Unlike health and education, housing is not a universal service. There may be social landlords in all parts of the country, and they may be providing a similar level of service, but this service is not a comprehensive one in terms of whom it is targeted at. Indeed, since its inception in the early twentieth century social housing has been targeted at those on low incomes rather than being aimed at all at the point of need, as is the National Health Service (King, 2001, 2003; King and Oxley, 2000). Social housing, then, has always been particularist and not aimed at housing all members of society. At its height in 1976 social housing catered for only a third of households and by 2004 had declined to around a fifth. This can be compared with health and education, where state provision accounts for around nine out of ten households.

This situation has not arisen by accident, but rather relates to the intrinsic qualities of housing provision compared with other essential welfare goods and, in particular, the ability an individual has to make informed choices about the consumption of these goods. Both housing and healthcare are expensive goods, and therefore there is the need for some planning, be it at the level of the household, providers, intermediary bodies or the state, to ensure that there is sufficient provision. They are also both crucial to human flourishing, and one's quality of life would be seriously diminished were there to be a serious lack of either. But the considerable differential in the levels of state provision would indicate that cost is not the main issue with regard to the nature of provision. I would argue that the key distinction relates to the amount of knowledge we have as individuals of our requirements with regard to these services (King, 2003). As individuals we may lack the requisite knowledge of the benefits to ourselves and others of consuming goods such as healthcare at a higher level. In this case, it is argued that government should subsidise the good to increase its provision.

While this argument can be readily applied to healthcare, the position regarding housing is less clear cut (King, 1998). One can know that one is ill and in pain, but not know the cause of the pain or the proper treatment that is required. One has to rely on an expert to diagnose and treat the ailment. One can seldom rely on past knowledge to assist one, and even if one could, one would still lack the expertise to treat the problem. Thus so-called information asymmetries can develop. Additionally, the need for healthcare is contingent on circumstances and is often unpredictable, in that we do not know when and if we will be ill. All these issues create problems for comprehensive market provision. There may be a tendency for there to be under-provision in such systems, particularly among the poor, who may choose to spend their limited resources elsewhere (King and Oxley, 2000).

The situation relating to housing, however, is significantly different (see Box 1). First, housing need is permanent, as we always need warmth, shelter, etc. (King, 1998). What differs, of course, is whether it is currently fulfilled. Second, this creates a

> **Box 1 Why housing is amenable to choice**
> 1 Housing need is permanent, as we always need housing
> 2 It is therefore predictable, allowing for a more regular
>   pattern of provision
> 3 Housing is more readily understandable, in that we know
>   we need it, that we will always need it, and to what
>   standard we require it

high degree of predictability, allowing for a more regular pattern of provision. Third, as a result, housing is more readily understandable without the need for professional intervention. Because housing has these qualities of permanence and predictability we know we need it, that we will always need it, and to what standard we require it (King, 1998, 2001, 2003). What this suggests is that, for housing, decision-making can be devolved to the level of the household and thus housing is more amenable to choice than healthcare. This does not have to mean that we can build or maintain it ourselves, but rather that we have sufficient knowledge to set the parameters and determine what we need.

This suggests that decision-making can be devolved to the level of the household and thus that housing is more amenable to choice.

This discussion helps us to come to some definition of what social housing is and what is meant by choice. This is particularly relevant to the discussion of the role of government and social landlords and the ability of households to determine their own affairs. Oxley and Smith (1996) state that social housing can be defined as housing that has been constructed from public funds and so rents are subsidised so that it can be provided at a price that it not principally determined by the profit motive, but is rather allocated according to some concept of need and where political decision making has an important influence in terms of the quantity, quality and terms of provision. The provision of social housing is therefore predicated on the basis that decision-making is taken away from the household.

In other words, social housing can be defined as the form of housing where it is deemed inappropriate to leave key decisions to the choices of either landlords or households rather than making them on a political or social[1] basis. We can define choice as:

> Where we are able to select from alternatives, even if the alternative is an either/or between two less than perfect solutions. It further implies we are able to make a preference and thus distinguish between entities, and that we are able to proffer reasons for the choices we make ... Choice is deemed to be a *capability* that individuals and households have, whereby they can materially affect their situation. It is where individuals take control over the decisions affecting them. (Brown and King, 2005: 66)

The issue about social housing in relation to choice, therefore, is where decision-making is located: just *who* is it who is capable of taking the key decisions affecting the housing situation of the household?

---

1   There are certainly writers who would object to the word 'social' being used here – one can almost hear F. A. Hayek say, 'What is a non-social house?' It is now clear from our analysis that so-called 'social housing' is housing over which there is a large degree of political control. I will continue to use the phrase 'social housing' because it has been absorbed into the language and thus helps clarity of exposition. I will use it to describe housing provided by local authorities, housing associations and other similar bodies.

What this discussion of epistemic conditions suggests is that housing is amenable to choice and thus we have to question *why* it is that social housing exists in the manner that it does. Furthermore, the importance of this discussion is that it shows the possibilities and limits of any prescription for the reform of social housing. First, social housing is a minority sector and that situation is not likely to alter. Second, because of these three epistemic conditions we have identified, housing is particularly amenable to choice. Our need for housing is permanent and predictable and we can readily understand what we need in order to be well housed. In principle, then, most of us can find our housing for ourselves, and do. Third, it follows from this that social housing will always have to contend with owner occupation as the dominant tenure. The comparative position in which social housing finds itself will always outweigh its own attempts to reconfigure itself. Fourth, there are implications for the manner in which social housing is provided and supported. If households are capable of taking decisions about their needs, the level and nature of support they require from the state are different from those required for their healthcare and educational needs. This means that we need to consider how housing is subsidised and whether it is the most appropriate means of support.

Changing subsidies

Over the last 30 years the balance of housing subsidies in Britain has altered. What we have seen is a move away from subsidies towards social landlords aimed at encouraging them to build new dwellings, towards personalised housing supports in the form of tax expenditures and housing allowances. Table 1 shows the impact of these changes.

Table 1 **Moving from object to subject subsidies (Great Britain)**

	1980/81	*2003/04*
Housing benefit	£0.4 bn	£12.6 bn
MITR*	£2.2 bn	–
Subtotal	**£2.6 bn (43%)**	**£12.6 bn (67%)**
Gross social housing investment	£4.0 bn (57%)	£6.2 bn (33%)
Total	**£6.6 bn**	**£18.8 bn**

* Mortgage interest tax relief

Source: Wilcox (2005)

In 1980/81 over half of housing subsidies were in the form of direct payments to landlords, whereas in 2003/04 this had fallen to a third. The purpose of these bricks-and-mortar or *object* subsidies is to encourage social landlords to build new dwellings. The main effect of these subsidies, therefore, is to increase the *supply* of housing. Clearly their decline in real terms indicates a reduced priority being given to increasing the scale of social housing. Rather the emphasis is now on subsidies to individual households, and this forms two-thirds of expenditure even after the abolition of mortgage interest tax relief. These personal or *subject* subsidies aim to make housing more affordable by increasing household income. They therefore have the effect of increasing the *demand* for housing.

What is interesting is that this shift in emphasis was mirrored in other developed economies in Europe and Australasia, with some countries such as Australia and New Zealand shifting almost entirely to subject subsidies. Kemp (1997) suggests three reasons for this general shift away from capital subsidies:

- The end of massive housing shortages meant that a reassessment of the housing problem was needed. The census in 1981 showed a crude surplus of dwellings in the UK and this situation was matched in other European countries (Power, 1993). Accordingly, the key housing problem was now seen not as a shortage of housing but of income on the part of a minority who could not afford good-quality housing.

- The belief that the welfare state was unaffordable in its current form. The economic problems experienced by Britain and other countries in the 1970s meant we could no longer support the burgeoning cost of welfare.
- A general belief in market solutions to problems in social and public policy emphasising the importance of the consumer over the producer of services.

So in general terms we can suggest that this change in the balance between object and subject subsidies implies a change in the purpose of housing subsidies. Instead of subsidy being used to increase supply, it is now aimed at bolstering demand.[2] The belief is that there is enough housing for the number of households in the country. What has been the issue for the last twenty years, therefore, is not the *quantity* of housing, but whether all households can gain *access to housing of sufficient quality*.

This situation has been developed somewhat by some of the issues we considered in Chapter 1 (and will return to in Chapter 5). The rising concern about local or regional shortages and the perceived need to deal with low demand in other areas now form a significant part of policy. Yet, as Table 1 shows, this has not altered

---

2   This is not to deny that increasing demand through subsidies does not have an effect on supply. As a result of planning restrictions, however, the effect may be indirect and insubstantial. Thus the demand-side subsidies give purchasing power to poorer households to purchase housing from a given stock.

the balance of expenditure between the two forms of subsidy, and the government spending plans do little to alter this balance.

What is significant here is that the two different forms of subsidy are based on two different sets of assumptions about the role of government and the competence of individual households. It is therefore worthwhile exploring some of these assumptions, as this will link into our discussion of the culture of social housing and help us to relate any reform proposals to past thinking on housing.

The purpose of object subsidies

Throughout much of the twentieth century the main form of housing support was in the form of object subsidies. We can suggest that this was largely aimed at dealing with housing short-ages, but there are also a number of general arguments given by economists and others seeking to justify this form of subsidy.

Housing is a merit good

Perhaps the most common such argument is that housing is a merit good and it is therefore socially desirable to provide good-quality housing. Merit goods can be defined as 'goods which society believes individuals should have but which some individuals decide not to purchase' (Oxley and Smith, 1996: 11). Oxley and Smith go on to relate this to housing provision by suggesting that 'Good quality housing can be viewed as a merit good which will bring benefits to individuals over and above those which individuals perceive' (p. 11) and that 'There is a case for governments encouraging the provision of merit goods which will inevitably be under-provided in a market system' (p. 11). Merit goods are therefore goods that individuals ought to consume at a certain level, because it is good for them. They may, however, not be fully aware of their benefits, or may choose not to consume to the desired level. Thus there might be a discrepancy between what individuals wish to do and what society as a whole thinks is best. Therefore, according to this argument, there might still be a problem even if individuals received money for themselves with which to purchase or rent houses – they may not use the money to purchase sufficiently 'good-quality' housing.

The problem with this view is that the problem is precisely not a matter of knowledge but of income. As we have discussed already, one of the important issues with regard to housing is that, except in a very few limited cases, people are eminently able to determine what it is we need. The problem is that some households may not be able to gain access to it on their current income. The issue for society, therefore, becomes one of determining whether the income of households should be supplemented and to what level.

Political acceptability

A further common argument, although perhaps heard less often now, is that housing consumption is politically acceptable, whereas a cash payment, which could be used for such things as alcohol and tobacco, might not be. As a society we approve of certain activities as being legitimate for subsidy, but not others. Thus we should ensure that public money is spent on things that benefit individuals and not merely on wants and desires.

But were we to accept this argument we would offer no cash

benefits whatsoever and merely offer clothing vouchers, food parcels and so on to those who are not well off. Clearly society feels comfortable offering benefits and pensions to its citizens and feels sanguine about their competence to spend them wisely. The same ought to apply to housing if, as we believe, individuals are capable of making decisions for themselves about how they spend their income.

We can point to a linked argument, which states that it is not fair to allow people on low income to make choices that can affect them disproportionately compared with those on reasonable incomes. Thus to give individuals a housing allowance and tell them to pay their rent as well as food, school uniform, transport and fuel bills is to set them up to fail. Therefore, the argument runs, it is better to provide houses rather than housing allowances.

What appears to lie at the heart of these arguments is that it is believed that certain people, who are often on the lowest incomes, cannot be trusted to spend their money wisely and need to have things provided for them by government. Yet it is unclear why income and competence are so linked, such that as soon as a person gains an income for themselves (i.e. starts working and earns above levels at which they receive income from the state) they suddenly become competent to decide for themselves. The problem with these arguments, therefore, is to justify why people can be competent when their incomes rise but incompetent when poor, and thus need specialist provision.

Links to wider social and political problems

Another argument is that poor-quality housing can lead to wider societal problems such as ill health, vandalism, racism, family break-up, etc. If people live in poor-quality housing they may become ill, or if there is a shortage of suitable housing in an area it might stir up racial tensions if some groups believe they are being excluded and others given preferential treatment. The point is that housing can have far-reaching effects, which go beyond fulfilling the wants of individual households. Housing provision, or the lack of it, can have social effects, and it is difficult for individuals to deal with these problems themselves. Therefore, it is suggested that building more social housing and to a high standard can help to deal with these social problems.

Yet one only has to look at where many of these social problems occur to realise that there are difficulties here. According to Brown and Passmore (1998), one of the three targets of the government's Social Exclusion Unit when it was established in 1997 was 'problem housing estates – its prime targets are the worst 1,370 *social housing estates* identified by a range of indicators of deprivation ...' (p. 123, my emphasis). This unit was specific- ally set up to deal with the consequences of poverty and multiple deprivation, such as high crime, racism, unemployment, low educational attainment and so on. Yet one of the main indicators of social exclusion was not private housing or the role of markets, but social housing estates. It therefore appears to be the case that building social housing can be as much a cause of social and polit- ical problems as their solution.

Cost differentials

A more technical argument for object subsidies is that, because of the differences in land and property values across the country, there are differential costs in a rental market and these can be ironed out by the provision of social housing at controlled rent levels. By subsidising the production of social housing, even if it means paying higher levels of subsidy to landlords in high-cost areas, rents can be similar across the country. This, it is argued, can encourage labour mobility as well as being seen to be fair and just.

But this argument would pertain only if social housing were free or available at much lower rents than have ever been the case in the UK. Currently over 60 per cent of social housing tenants are in receipt of housing benefit as they are unable to afford their rent without a housing allowance. Indeed, council housing became truly open to the very poorest only once housing allowances were introduced in 1972 (King, 2001). This suggests that object subsidies would need to be considerably higher per dwelling than has been the case, and that social landlords should receive a higher level of revenue subsidy to assist them in managing and maintaining their stock of dwellings.

But, of course, there is no reason why the logic of differential costs cannot apply to a housing allowance system. The current housing benefit system in the UK is based on actual rents and thus payments differ between high- and low-rent areas. The net effect of this on household access is no different from that of paying different levels of subsidy to allow landlords to build in these areas.

Benefit take-up

It can be argued that, as the take-up for a housing allowance will inevitably be below 100 per cent, some people will miss out on what they are entitled to. This might be because some people are unaware of their entitlements, or because they perceive a stigma attached to handouts from the state. Thus it might be best to fund housing providers to ensure that good-quality housing is available without the need for households to claim benefits.

Government admits, however, that this is not an issue with housing benefit, which has consistently had a take-up rate of over 97 per cent. This is because for the majority of recipients housing benefit is paid directly to the landlord, who consequently has an incentive to ensure it is fully claimed. Claiming for housing benefit is a well-ingrained habit for the vast majority, and we can presume that this would remain so under another system.

But more generally the use of this argument to support object subsidies needs to deal with why there is low demand for social housing in some areas: either it is not wanted by the local population or it was the result of bad central and local planning. Allied to the existence of waiting lists in other parts of the country, this indicates that social housing is not a particularly effective means of dealing with demand in any case.

Poverty trap

A problem associated with subject subsidies is that they can create a poverty or employment trap because individuals are reluctant to take low-paid work because of the way in which their benefits are withdrawn as their income rises. For instance, under current housing benefit regulations, 65 pence of benefit is withdrawn for every extra pound a claimant earns. When one takes into account the increasing tax and National Insurance paid as earnings increase, one can see how one might be better off on benefit. It can therefore be argued that providing the goods 'in kind', in the form of social housing, would help to deal with this problem.

But, as have already seen, a majority of social housing tenants can afford their housing only because they receive a subject subsidy. For this argument to hold, then, rents would have to be zero. This would then raise the question, 'How is entitlement to social housing reduced as income rises?' Another poverty trap might simply be created.[3] Alternatively, there would have to be other ways or rationing social housing found – all of which would place arbitrary powers in the hands of politicians and council officers. We can also question the wisdom and expense of subsidising rents on social housing to zero. We also need to appreciate that for many it might not just be a matter of benefits harming labour mobility and access to employment, but the fact that social housing can be hard to access and once attained the household may be reluctant to give it up, even if their job prospects are better elsewhere. The differential demand for social housing in different parts of the country can therefore be as much of a drag on labour mobility as are house prices (Clapham, 2005).

Controlling subsidies

One great advantage of object subsidies, for government if no one else, is that they can allow for greater control over the quality of housing provided for low-income households. By providing subsidies to a particular level, and applying a particular control and monitoring regime, government can ensure the quality of outcomes. Conversely, it can also ensure that recipients do not

3   See below under 'Targeting' – if social housing is not withdrawn as income increases it is occupied by people who do not need it.

benefit excessively from public funds. A key problem with housing allowance systems such as housing benefit which have general eligibility criteria, however, is that government cannot control the number of recipients and therefore the level of expenditure. Government can limit entitlements and eligibility, but this is less fine-grained than the control it can have over object subsidies, where it can much more accurately set the limits of funding.

This is the reason, of course, why successive governments have not totally abandoned object subsidies. But while some might consider this a strong argument, we can question whether controlling systems is sufficient justification for a form of subsidy. The purpose of subsidies is not to allow government to control social landlords, but to assist certain households deemed to be in need. At best this can therefore only be a subsidiary argument and not something that should be seen as the basis for keeping one system or another. Indeed, if control were the sole basis for housing subsidies, we could surely come up with a housing allowance system that disbursed a pre-determined number of vouchers operated through a needs-based allocation system. But this is again not what we perhaps naively consider that housing subsidies exist to do.

Incentives to build

A final argument for object subsidies is that they act as direct incentives to supply new housing. It was argued that if one has a shortage of housing, as had been the case in most Western countries throughout the last century,[4] subsidising landlords is the

---

4   It could be argued that the word 'shortage' has no particular meaning in this context as price will adjust to equilibrate supply and demand. In response, however,

most direct and effective way of getting houses built. But it also encourages quality by allowing landlords to build to a higher standard than they might if left to a market where they would perhaps be more concerned with covering their costs and making a profit based on the limitations of the budgets of the households to which the houses would be let.

But this again presupposes that government is able to plan effectively and efficiently where developments should occur. We have already seen that the government is having to deal with low-demand areas, and this has included the demolition of new social housing developments (Bramley and Pawson, 2002). The problem with this housing was not its quality, merely that no one wanted it. But, as we saw with the discussion of the Social Exclusion Unit above, government and social landlords do not necessarily have a terribly good record in building popular and good-quality housing. And, to reiterate the point, the majority of applicants in these dwellings can afford to live there only because they receive housing benefit. Indeed, a key test of the viability of a new social housing scheme is whether it can be made to break even based on 100 per cent housing benefit uptake. We can therefore argue that a key incentive to build is the existence of a comprehensive system of subject subsidies.

Arguments for subject subsidies

The above section has rehearsed some of the main arguments

---

it can be said that there have been institutional factors (notably the planning system) and also housing damage in World War II which have meant that differences between supply and demand have tended to be met by price adjustments in the market with quantity being more sluggish to respond.

used to justify object subsidies and shown them to have considerable faults, both in their logic and based on their outcomes. The implication from this is that a system based on subject subsidies is to be preferred. This is indeed our purpose here, but this needs to be justified, and hence we need to understand some of the facets of subject subsidies more fully.

Producer capture

It is assumed that the purpose of subsidies is to help people in need. Yet on several occasions already in this discussion on social housing we have shown how subsidies are used to control provision. The questions we therefore need to consider are: who or what are subsidy systems for and do they benefit the producers of the service or the consumers (King, 1998)? It can be argued that object subsidies can be controlled by producers and operate to their benefit. If producers can control subsidies – because they are made through them – how can we ensure that consumers are being treated properly and that provision is being made efficiently and fairly?

One way of examining this issue is through the arguments of public choice theory. Boyne et al. (2003) suggest that public choice theory is based upon three main criticisms of the role of public organisations. First, they suggest that many public services are provided by monopoly suppliers, either at the national level, such as the NHS, or locally, such as local authority housing departments. Public monopoly can lead to poor performance because officials have little incentive to keep costs down or innovate. There are few financial or other benefits for those who innovate and resources are not directed by the users but by a 'political' sponsor.

Therefore officials are more likely to respond to political pressure than to that from customers.

Second, there is an absence of valid indicators of organisational performance by which to judge outcomes and ensure that consumers' interests are uppermost. Public choice theorists suggest that there are no unambiguous indicators in the public sector, making it difficult to evaluate individual or collective performance. Third, the large size of public organisations creates problems of coordination and control, and these lead to a decline in performance as the size of the organisation increases. In response to these issues public choice theorists advocate a more competitive structure with rivalries within the public sector, and between public and private sectors. This would force greater information sharing to judge performance and would break up large agencies into smaller units. They also suggest that consumers be given some level of choice to determine their supplier and the level of service they receive. The most direct manner of achieving this is through the use of vouchers for services or by directing subsidies to the consumers themselves, thus forcing producers to compete for their custom.

We need to appreciate, however, that subject subsidies are not necessarily immune to producer capture, and the housing benefit system is an example of this. So long as private and social housing providers were able to set their own rents they were able to use housing benefit as a further form of revenue subsidy. This is because of the heavy dependence on housing benefit of tenants, and the method of direct payment to landlords, which means that tenants are largely unaffected by, and unaware of, changes in rent levels. The reforms to the housing benefit system that are currently under way are intended to deal with this, and this suggests that the problem here is one of system design. Thus it is possible to design a housing allowance system not prone to producer capture: it is difficult, however, to imagine a system of object subsidies that would be so immune.

Targeting

One of the main justifications for subject subsidies is that they can be targeted to those in need and can be withdrawn when income increases. Households allocated a council house can stay there all their lives, regardless of how their income and personal circumstances change. Thus needy low-income households might be denied access to social housing because more affluent households remain in occupation, even though they might now be able to afford owner occupation or private renting. A system of subject subsidies, however, could prevent this because households would be subsidised according to their current circumstances and not their past. The subsidy can thus be withdrawn if and when their circumstances change. Interestingly, the city of Rotterdam in the Netherlands is beginning a policy of means-testing tenancies with the aim of ensuring that households whose income reaches beyond a certain point do not remain in social housing.

Increase in tenants' negotiating strength

It could be argued that object subsidies give too dominant a role to landlords at the expense of tenants. Landlords are able to exercise control over rents and the level of service offered to tenants. Paying subsidies to tenants, however, gives them some negotiating strength over rent levels. It would create a different and more equal relationship between landlord and tenant. This is, as the UK system demonstrates, dependent upon system design.

Tenure neutrality

Even though the housing benefit system excludes owner occupation and treats social and private tenants differently, a further advantage given for subject subsidies is that they can be tenure neutral, in that they can be applied to all housing sectors, including owner occupation. Subject subsidy systems can be devised that are so designed as to allow access to all and which can be dependent only on income rather than tenure or any particular relationship with the state.

Stigma

In discussing object subsidies we raised the issue of stigma and suggested that this might be a reason for preferring subsidies to landlords instead of handouts to tenants. Perhaps a generation ago this might indeed have been a considerable problem, with many households being reluctant to go 'on the dole' or receive a handout.

The issue of stigma, however, is now more relevant to social housing, as the National Housing Federation's 'rebranding' exercise shows. Owner occupation is now so much the dominant tenure that there is perceived to be a fault with those who have not achieved it and must rely on state-provided housing. It could be argued that this stigma could be avoided to a certain extent by giving individual payments, allowing households to purchase or rent privately. It may well be the case, however, that the stigma attached to social housing is now so ingrained as to be irreversible. Perhaps we should see the Blair government's pursuit of low-income owner occupation in this light.

No links between subsidies and quality

While the supporters of object subsidies argue that they help landlords to build good-quality housing, there is no automatic link between this form of subsidy and quality outputs (even where there is sufficient demand for the dwellings). Local authorities and housing associations have been guilty of building poor-quality and unpopular housing (Page, 1993; Power, 1987). Local authorities were encouraged by the subsidy system in the 1950s and 1960s to build high-rise blocks, which are not universally popular and, as with the example of Ronan Point in 1968, have proved on occasions to be disastrous.

Unbalanced communities

Developing this point on the nature of the outcomes of state provision, it can be argued that object subsidies have led to ghettoisation and unbalanced communities (Marsland, 1996). They have created large estates where many of the occupants are economically inactive and where those who can afford to leave do so. As a result, social housing has become a key indicator of social exclusion.

Choice

But perhaps the most significant benefit to be derived from

a subject subsidy system is that it can offer households some choice over where they live and the type of accommodation they wish to reside in. Paying the subsidy directly to households enables them to exercise more control over their lives than if the subsidy were paid to landlords who built where and what they felt was required. As we have seen several times already, the issue of system design is crucial here, as in Britain much of the housing benefit paid out goes directly to the landlord, which detracts from this particular advantage of subject subsidies. But this is not a necessary part of the system and could be remedied by a change in policy. One can suggest that the current proposals to reform housing benefit seek to do this, mainly by ending direct payments to landlords.

Paying benefit directly to individual households enables them to have some choice over their housing, which is not open to households in an object subsidy system. Of course, this does not mean that households have an untrammelled choice or that their options are limitless. This is used as a criticism of choice-based systems, in that because choice is not limitless, and indeed in practice might be quite limited, it is somehow an illusion. Yet the choices open to most households are limited, being hemmed in by income and family ties, employment opportunities, available schools and the quality of public transport, even before we get to issues such as housing supply and availability. What we have to remember is that choice does not have to be limitless still to be choice.

This discussion on subsidies has shown that housing is amenable to choice, and that this applies regardless of income and tenure. This suggests that we should not seek to deny choice to social housing tenants. These choices will not be limitless, and some people will have more choice than others. But whatever the level, it is an improvement on the centralised and bureaucratic modes of provision that have dominated British housing for the last 50 years.

3   HOW WE GOT TO WHERE WE ARE

Housing systems are seldom purpose built, but have developed piecemeal over time. This means that they can be hard to understand and very complicated: it is not clear why things are as they appear. This can be an excuse not to change things, the fear of getting things wrong being greater than the opportunities opened up by successful reform. One way of dealing with this fear is to try to chart a path through the complex interrelationships of policies to come to some understanding of how we got to our current predicament. In order to understand current systems, therefore, we need to appreciate how we acquired them. What I wish to do in this chapter is to consider some of the important issues in the development of housing policy. This will, of necessity, be brief and far from inclusive. My aim is rather to show those developments and policies which, with the benefit of hindsight, can be seen as particularly significant.

This brief historical study shows that we have moved from a market-dominated housing system with only light government regulation to one dominated by government activity and the desire by the centre to control the activity of housing providers. Yet what is also clear is that a majority still provide for themselves through a market. This shows the resilience of housing markets, and points to the fundamental amenability of housing to choice and individual decision-making which we highlighted in the previous chapter.

The early years

At the start of World War I nearly 90 per cent of households were in private rented accommodation, with most of the remainder being owner-occupiers. We can characterise this as a market relatively free of government regulation. Within a year of the war starting, however, a policy had been put in train which fundamentally altered this tenure pattern irrevocably. The war had the effect of creating huge shifts in the population as a large number of active males went abroad to fight, leaving gaps in the labour force at a time of heightened industrial production. There was therefore an influx of the population into urban areas. The need to prioritise production for the war effort, however, meant that there was a shortage of building materials, and this meant that there was no new building during the period of the war.

This led in 1915 to significant increases in rents in many large cities, owing to a combination of increased demand and the impossibility of increasing supply. As a result there were a number of rent strikes in key industrial areas, such as Glasgow, that were crucial to the war effort. In response the government introduced the Increase of Rent and Mortgage Interest (War Restrictions) Act 1915, which fixed rents and interest rates on mortgages at their August 1914 levels. This Act had the effect of defusing rent levels as a crisis issue and, as an emergency measure, it was intended to be repealed once the war ended. The Act imposed a rent ceiling for most rented housing.

The aim of rent control was to make housing cheaper. While it was intended to act as a subsidy to tenants, however, it did not operate in the same way as subsidies now used by government, such as housing benefit and the Social Housing Grant. While government insisted on the measure, it did not itself fund the

Table 2 **The decline in private renting in the UK**

Year	% of households renting from private landlords
1914	89
1945	53
1961	31
1971	18.9
1981	11.1
1991	9.4
2001	9.7

Source: Malpass and Murie (1999); Wilcox (2005)

subsidies to tenants. This cost fell on landlords, who were unable to increase rents, and thus their income dropped even when their expenditure had increased. The consequences of this were dramatic in that it altered the incentive structures operating within rented housing markets. Rents were lower than they would otherwise have been, leading to an increase in demand. Landlords could not increase rents, however, which reduced their ability to maintain and improve their properties and, after the war ended, gave them no incentive to increase supply to match the increased demand. Indeed, as Table 2 demonstrates, over time landlords found it more advantageous to leave the market or to use other techniques to enhance their income, such as illegal letting, the use of key money and harassment (Albon and Stafford, 1987). The result was a distorted market of cheap rents and poor levels of supply both in terms of numbers and, increasingly, the quality of the stock.

The 1915 Act can be seen as significant for two reasons. First, it was important because it was the first time government had actively intervened in property rights in a proscriptive (rather than permissive) manner to try to manage housing provision and consumption. Second, it showed that government action has unintended consequences, because, once the Act was in place, it became politically difficult to repeal. The housing shortage merely worsened at the end of the war in 1919 as millions of soldiers returned and started families. While attempts to amend or repeal the Act were made in the 1920s and 1930s, it was never fully repealed until the 1950s.[1] The intention of rent controls was the entirely understandable one of protecting tenants, but the net effect was to contribute to the long-term decline in the private rented sector. Landlords were unable to increase income in line with increases in expenditure and the cost of purchasing property, and thus found it harder to improve and maintain their properties. As a result many landlords took the opportunity to leave the market and invest their capital elsewhere.

But rent controls did nothing to deal with vagrancy and poor conditions. Indeed, by reducing supply they merely made them worse. Government, as many on the left had been urging since the 1880s, began to look to more direct methods both to increase the total housing stock and to improve its quality. This involved the first attempt at direct government subsidy in the so-called Addison Act of 1919. This introduced government subsidies to local authorities, which would cover the liability on any debts incurred above a penny rate contribution. This was a generous system and the resulting houses were of a good quality. In 1923 this subsidy was altered to a fixed subsidy, whereby a local authority received £X per dwelling for Y years. This formula for subsidy remained intact until 1972, with only the level of X and Y altering when government tried to either encourage more development or to reduce expenditure.

---

1   While the Act was repealed in the 1950s, its basic measures and effects continued.

The inter-war period also saw an increase in owner occupation, particularly in the 1930s, which was a period of rising real incomes, static house prices and the development of building societies as sources for secure and stable investments with a high degree of liquidity. The result was a boom in owner occupation fuelled by competition among building societies flush with funds. Thus the biggest-growing sector in the inter-war years was not local authority housing but owner occupation. Indeed, the boom in owner occupation in the 1930s occurred during a period when subsidies to local authorities were substantially cut (Boddie, 1992).

1945 and after

The issues facing government in the immediate post-war period were a chronic shortage of housing caused by war damage and an inability to build, compounded by a rise in demand created by an increase in household formation and a baby boom. Therefore one of the priorities for Attlee's Labour government in 1945 was to start building housing as quickly as possible. Its chosen method in doing this was not to open up the housing market, but to maintain rigid building controls and to further develop subsidy mechanisms put in place in the 1920s and 1930s. Consequently, the 25 years following World War II were a period of massive expansion of council housing. Despite some attempts to reduce subsidy and decontrol rents in the late 1950s, the Conservatives largely went along with this policy of building council houses. Council house building never fell below 150,000 per annum throughout the 1950s and remained in excess of 80,000 right through to the end of the 1970s. One can therefore suggest that there was a considerable consensus around the issue of dealing with a shortage of dwellings, which was to be met by mass council building.

But government subsidy can also be used to influence the type of housing as well as the overall number of dwellings. This can be seen in the Housing Repairs and Rents Act 1954, which encouraged slum clearance and private sector improvement, while the Housing Act 1956 offered higher subsidies for high-rise building. Thus government used the subsidy system to encourage local authorities to build certain types of dwellings.

There are two significant points to be made here. First, governments have always attempted to direct local authorities (and more recently housing associations) through targeted subsidies. Social landlords have never been left to determine their own priorities, but have been directed to a greater or lesser extent by central government. Second, one merely has to look at the aftermath of the 1956 Act, with its encouragement of high-rise housing, to see that the effects of housing subsidies are long-term. Housing is a long-lived asset, and while this means that it can provide a long-term benefit, it also shows that the liabilities hang around for a considerable period too. When mistakes are made by government in housing they can be expensive, long-lasting and large-scale. Direct intervention and object subsidies are more likely to give rise to such mistakes.

The 1970s and the end of consensus

While the 1960s were largely a period of consolidation, with some increase in tenants' rights and security of tenure, the 1970s saw the beginning of some quite fundamental changes, which are still being felt now. In particular, the period saw major changes in the operation of housing subsidies. The economic problems that became manifest in the 1970s, with the economy being plagued by high inflation and increasing unemployment simultaneously, led to cuts in the council house building programme and the attempt by both the Heath and Callaghan governments to impose greater controls. Thus the 1970s are important because this period saw a change in emphasis away from the encouragement of council house building and towards the limitation of development to match government public spending targets.

The first signal of this change in policy came as early as 1972 when Heath's Conservative government introduced radical reforms to housing finance, changing the capital funding system that had operated since 1923. The Housing Finance Act 1972 undertook a fundamental reform of housing subsidies, ending government's long-term commitment to fund council house building and replacing it with a deficit revenue subsidy.[2] It also sought to gain greater leverage over rents. But the most significant reform of the 1972 Act was the introduction of a mandatory rent rebate scheme for council tenants and tenants in non-furnished private rented accommodation.[3] The significance of this change was that ability to pay was no longer a bar on access to council housing. Over time this change, when taken together with policies such as the Right to Buy, and the homelessness provisions introduced in

---

2   Prior to the 1972 Act council housing development was funded by long-term subsidies that offered a certain amount of money per dwelling for a fixed number of years. These fixed subsidies were replaced by an annual subsidy aimed at balancing income and expenditure incurred in managing and maintaining the council's housing stock. The significance of this was that government had replaced a long-term commitment with an annual one. See the discussion on p. 55 above.

3   Rent rebates were offered to council tenants on low incomes. Rent allowances were offered to tenants in the private and housing association sectors. The two systems were brought together into the current housing benefit system in 1982.

1977, has had the effect of changing the demographic make-up of council tenants, away from a dominance of the affluent working classes and towards those who are economically inactive.

The importance of the 1972 Act then, was, first, that it gave government a mechanism with which to control activity, and second, that it saw the start of the move away from object subsidies to subject subsidies. We can see this particular piece of legislation as the point at which the shift away from government's encouragement of building and towards controlling activity began. This shift in emphasis was heightened with the introduction in 1977/78 of the requirement for local authorities to submit Housing Investment Programmes detailing their assessment of housing need and a costed programme of works for housing capital expenditure. This was initially presented as a means for rational planning, whereby scarce resources could be matched to the most pressing local needs, but it developed in the 1980s and 1990s into a further means of central control. Government achieved this by establishing the priorities under which local authorities must bid for funds.

Housing associations also achieved more recognition and state support with the Housing Act 1974, which gave the Housing Corporation the powers to make grants to associations which covered most of the costs of development. From 1974 housing associations began to grow in significance as social landlords, to the extent that the Thatcher government could place them at the centre of policy from 1988 onwards.

The 1970s also saw the end of the consensus that had largely existed in housing policy since the late 1940s. This became clear in 1979 after the election of the Conservative government, which began to shift away from a public sector solution, instead seeing council housing as the problem. Policy was shifted more towards the promotion of owner occupation. While it is the case that most post-war governments, including Attlee's, elected in 1945, promoted owner occupation as a desirable tenure, all these governments did so alongside a policy of mass public house building. Most governments saw owner occupation as an important aspiration for middle-class and, from the 1960s onwards, working-class households. Yet this did not detract from their support for publicly rented housing.

The Thatcher government elected in 1979, however, took a somewhat different view, seeing the two tenures as competing rather than complementing each other. As a result, after 1979 local authorities lost their position at the centre of housing policy and saw their stock decline, owing to a shift in subsidies. But also by the end of the 1970s politicians could claim that the crude shortfall in dwellings had been met and therefore the key housing problem was no longer that of shortage but of quality.

Conservative housing policy in the 1980s and 1990s

The main plank of Conservative housing policy in the 1980s and 1990s was promotion of owner occupation as a tenure offering choice and independence from state interference. The government also increasingly saw local authorities as the cause of housing problems, rather than the solution to them. Therefore one can characterise government policy as pursuing an increase in owner occupation at the expense of local authority housing. Of course, the primary example of this policy is the Right to Buy, which allows existing council (and some housing association) tenants to purchase the house in which they live at a discount. But the

Conservatives also made some major changes to the management of local authority housing finance through the Housing Act 1980 (see Chapter 4 for a fuller discussion of the impact of the Right to Buy).

The 1980 Act also reformed council housing revenue subsidies with the aim of further increasing the level of control exercised by central government. The aim of these changes was to force councils to operate according to the government's agenda by fixing subsidy levels according to government's assumptions on legitimate income (and therefore rent levels) and expenditure, rather than on actual spending by the council. The result was a reduction in subsidy and an increase in rents. By the end of the 1980s, however, the success of these reforms had presented the government with a dilemma. Subsidies had been reduced to such an extent that by 1987/88 only 95 of 374 local authorities were receiving subsidy. But when a local authority stopped being in receipt of subsidy, government lost any leverage it had over rents.

A further issue was that government was concerned with the growth in rent rebates and the consequent effect on public expenditure. Throughout the 1980s unemployment had been at relatively high levels compared with post-war experience. The government was also concerned with demographic trends such as the growth in elderly-person households, as well as the number of economically inactive social tenants. It was therefore eager to find some means whereby the cost of rent rebates could be minimised. The government also sought ways of controlling the large amounts of capital receipts that local authorities had accumulated as a result of council house sales.

The result of these deliberations was the Local Government and Housing Act 1989. The Act forced local authorities to use the majority of their capital receipts to pay off their debts, which, combined with the reduction in stock, had the benefit of reducing both the level of public debt and future subsidy liability. On the revenue side the Act brought together the existing housing deficit subsidy established in 1972 and rent rebate subsidies, which paid for the cost of housing benefit for council tenants. Bringing these two together brought all councils back into subsidy and hence the government regained leverage over them. In addition, merging the two subsidies allowed government to use control over income and expenditure to offset the cost of housing benefit. By assuming that income increased more rapidly than expenditure, and setting the deficit housing subsidy accordingly, many councils were soon running their housing revenue account at a nominal surplus. This surplus was used to offset entitlement to rent rebate subsidy, with the result that local rents began to be used to fund housing benefit payments at the local level. The effect of this change was such that since 1995/96 the level of the sum of the surpluses used to offset rent rebates has been greater than the total level of deficit subsidy paid out. The government has therefore been effectively running council housing at a profit since the mid-1990s.

But this legislation also led to another unintended consequence, when many councils started to plan means of subverting the 1989 Act by transferring their housing stock to newly established housing associations. This practice has indeed developed to the extent that 970,000 dwellings were transferred between 1988 and 2003 (Pawson, 2004). While this was initially intended to subvert government policy, it effectively suited the aims of the Conservative administration, which a year before had introduced legislation to assist council tenants who wanted to transfer to another landlord (see the discussion on 'Tenants' Choice' in

Chapter 4). In consequence, large-scale voluntary transfer quickly became regulated and controlled by the government, which imposed a levy on the resulting capital receipts and limited the numbers of properties to be transferred in any one year. As we shall see, stock transfer has developed as a policy to the extent that it is now effectively the cornerstone of government housing policy.

The piece of legislation establishing Tenants' Choice also altered the funding arrangements for housing associations. The system introduced in 1974 was effective in producing dwellings of a high quality at reasonable rents. It aimed to enable housing associations to cover the costs of a particular scheme from the first year's income from that scheme, with a grant made to cover the difference. The result was grant levels averaging around 80 per cent. From the government's perspective, however, it had a number of problems. Housing associations had no incentive to economise, especially as the grant level was set at the end of the development process, based on the fair rent set by the County Rent Officer. In addition, associations could claim revenue deficit subsidies if expenditure on a scheme was greater than rent income. So it was felt that housing associations were enjoying a very high level of subsidy where there was no relationship between rents and the development costs of the scheme owing to the manner in which rents were set. The Housing Act 1988 dealt with these problems by establishing pre-determined grant rates for new development at a fixed percentage of the costs of development. Housing associations would need to borrow from the private sector in order to fund the rest of the capital cost. In order to facilitate this dealing with the private sector, housing associations were given the power to set their own rents. This Act therefore finally saw the end of rent controls introduced in 1915. This liberalisation of rents and changes to tenancies also applied to the private rented sector with the aim of reinvigorating what had been in decline for nearly a century.

Since 1988 housing associations have been at the centre of housing policy as the main providers of new social housing. This has led to an expansion in the size of the housing associations sector from 608,000 dwellings in 1991 to 1,621,000 in 2003 (which, of course, includes the effect of stock transfer), but it has also led to a cultural change, with associations now seeing themselves much more as businesses rather than charities or welfare bodies. In terms of the impact on tenants, however, the 1988 changes saw a doubling of rents by 1996 (King, 2001) and a reduction in their rights, particularly with new tenants losing the Right to Buy.

Indeed, the changes brought in by the 1988 and 1989 Acts were in some ways counter-productive. In particular, the increases in private and social rents that arose directly out of the policy merely led to a dramatic rise in housing benefit costs. While the average annual increase in housing benefit in the 1980s had been 4 per cent, the increase between 1989 and 1996 was 11 per cent per annum. This the government found unsustainable, with the total cost of housing benefit increasing from £4 billion in 1988/89 to £12.2 billion in 1996/97, despite its attempt to restrict the liability in the 1989 Act (ibid.). As a result the government introduced a series of restrictions on the payment of rent rebate subsidy in the council sector and the restriction of entitlements and payments in the private sector. These changes can be seen as a form of administrative rent control (ibid.), whereby instead of legislation the government uses ad hoc methods to control rents.

This has been a rather intermittent historical survey, but the aim has been to pick out those policies that have had a lasting effect, or which determine policy-making at the present time. This coverage has sought to show how we got to where we are now and to reveal some of the ways in which the current government is hemmed in. But what I also think this brief historical overview shows is that government, once it began to intervene, has found it impossible to step back. Even the Conservatives in the 1990s found it impossible to allow markets to take their course. This may be for two reasons: it may be that housing markets do not work well; or it may be because government is simply not prepared to take the consequences of doing nothing and seeing how markets develop. But there may be a third reason: that successive governments, despite the resources at their disposal and the long history of intervention, simply do not understand what is important about housing and thus which policies work and which do not. In consequence, most housing policies are prey to unintended consequences and need to be changed within a short period of time. I want to develop this somewhat by considering what might be considered both the most important and the most successful housing policy of the post-war period. My purpose in doing so is to bring out just what it is that is important to us as households living in dwellings, and thus what policy can and cannot do. This will help us to assess current policies and those that we might want to propose for the future.

4 WHY SOME POLICIES SUCCEED AND OTHERS DO NOT

Having considered something of the context surrounding social housing, and before looking at current polices, I want to explore why some policies work and some do not. This is important because much of current policy-making rests on the notion of choice and the role of markets. There would appear, then, to be much to welcome in current policies. Yet I want to suggest that there is still something crucial that is missing, and until this element is added any policy is likely to fail.

'Putting people first'

The government's *Sustainable Communities* plan (ODPM, 2003) states 'We are putting people first' (p. 3). It is a plan determined to create communities and not just concentrate on the allocation of resources. Of course, this is somewhat undermined by the rest of the plan, which provides considerable detail on how resources are to be allocated and offers no mechanism for how 'people' are to be involved in this. Making statements like this is, of course, easy, and in most cases it is well-meaning nonsense. All governments claim to 'put people first'; how could they claim otherwise? Yet how much of housing policies past and present actually did so?

Indeed, more generally, just what does housing policy mean

to social housing tenants? Why do we think it affects them or helps them? Most housing polices are concerned with the ordering of structures and the way organisations arrange themselves, and therefore have no direct impact on tenants. The *Sustainable Communities* plan is no different in this regard, with its schemes to redirect subsidy and encourage the use of new delivery vehicles. The effect of this policy since 2003 has been an increase in housing association mergers and group structures, aiming to take advantage of economies of scale within a framework based on volume building in targeted locations. The changes have been at the level of housing organisations, and one wonders how many of the 'people' have actually noticed any changes.

But then, why should they? Social housing tenants, I hope it is not surprising to suggest, have the same view of their dwelling as anyone else. They imbue it with the same meaning and use it as their own, and rightly so. What matters to all households, regardless of their tenure, is the manner in which they are able to use their dwelling (King, 2004). It matters little from which policy this situation is derived and what the particular standing and status of their landlord is. Tenants, like all households, want a dwelling that works, which fulfils its functions, which they feel comfortable in, and which offers them security. There is a lot of distance between this sense of private enjoyment and the heady world of sustainable communities and 'step changes'.

So one thing housing policy does not do very well is precisely what the *Sustainable Communities* plan claims to be doing: 'putting people first'. If it were doing this it would not be concentrating on structures, but on the manner in which individual households are able to use their dwelling. Part of this involves how households are able to gain access to housing – and this is something the government has turned its attention to – but this is not enough in itself. What matters to most households, most of the time, is the manner in which they are able to use their property. I would suggest that there has been only one policy over the last 25 years that has focused on this aspect, and for that reason, for all its faults, it should be seen as the most successful housing policy of the postwar period. By looking at why this policy was so successful we can start to develop some means of analysing current policies and future proposals.

The Right to Buy and why it worked

Most housing commentators, academics and professionals were and still are opposed to the Right to Buy as a policy. It is criticised for its alleged effects (increased homelessness, residualisation and reduction in the quality of the housing stock); as a form of privatisation; and as being socially regressive, in that it benefited the more affluent tenants at the expense of the very poorest. Yet equally the Right to Buy can and should be seen as the most successful housing policy of the last 25 years, if success is to be measured by the closeness of outcomes to initial aims. Whether one agrees with the policy or not, it has certainly succeeded in broadening owner occupation, particularly to working-class households, and in breaking up municipal housing. Moreover, despite the weight of opinion against it and recent limits to discounts and qualifying periods, it is quite unthinkable that the Right to Buy could be abolished. Indeed, prior to the 2005 election there was much speculation that the Blair government intended to extend the policy to cover housing association tenants, and only the intransigence of the deputy prime minister, John Prescott, prevented this. We therefore have a policy that, no matter what criticism it may receive from academics and lobby groups, is so established that the political debate is still whether it should be *extended* and not whether it can be abolished. It is my view that it is not by coincidence that the Right to Buy has been so successful, and if we can understand why this is so, we might be able to judge what other policies might be successful and have a more general set of criteria to assess policy.

In trying to analyse the success of Right to Buy I want to compare it with another policy brought in by the Thatcher government, which was also intended to demunicipalise social housing: this policy was Tenants' Choice, which was introduced in 1989 and repealed in 1996. I believe it is instructive to examine why Tenants' Choice failed when the Right to Buy succeeded. Both these policies were intended to achieve the privatisation of housing and to diminish the stock of local authority dwellings, and give residents more control, yet only one of them could be said to have had any success in achieving these aims.

The reason for the divergent outcomes of these two policies, and this is pertinent to the more general question of housing policy failure, lies in the distinct, and mutually exclusive, perceptions of housing that underpinned these policies. The Right to Buy, which allows sitting tenants to buy their current dwelling at a discount, focuses attention on housing as a *private* entity. Tenants' Choice, however, which allowed council tenants as a group to vote for a new landlord, retained the perception of housing as primarily *public*. The Right to Buy altered the relationship between an individual household and its dwelling by vesting control with the household itself. Tenants' Choice, however, if it had actually been used,[1] would have left the relationship between dwelling and household unchanged, merely altering the landlord. The tenants would now be beholden to someone else, and the fact that they could choose to whom to be beholden would not materially affect their own level of control. Any power the tenants had would be lost as soon as they had voted; but this is precisely when the landlord's power over them would begin.

The distinction here, therefore, is that one policy concentrated on the use to which the household could put the dwelling – it became an asset and something the new owners could pass on to their children, use as collateral, sell for a profit, take a pride in owning, etc. – while the other was concerned with the ownership of a collection of dwellings. One policy, through allowing households to exercise greater control, succeeded, while the other failed to capture the imagination of tenants, largely because it would not change anything beyond whom they paid their rent to. The essence of the Right to Buy as a successful policy, therefore, was the fact that it played on the private relationship between a household and the dwelling: it concentrated on the facility with which the actors could control their environment, whereas the change in ownership as part of Tenants' Choice would make no difference to the private relationship the tenants had with their dwellings.

So what is significant about the Right to Buy over and above all other policies is the increased level of control experienced by the household. Their subjective experience of the dwelling has been altered because they are now able to exert a more fundamental influence over their dwelling environment, including even when to change it by moving to a new dwelling. The dwelling has

---

1   Only one transfer took place in the London Borough of Westminster before the policy was repealed in 1996.

therefore been privatised, in that it is no longer legitimate for the public to have an interest in it: it is now the sole responsibility of the resident household to maintain it, pay for it and determine its use. People will put different subjective values on their dwelling, even though it may not differ greatly from their neighbours'. These differences in value can be substantial, but they can be realised only when the dwelling is privately owned.

Can social housing ever succeed?

The above consideration of the Right to Buy might be seen as rather abstract in comparison with the everyday cut and thrust of policy. But I would suggest that it is of primary importance in appreciating not just past policies, but the future direction of policies. The Right to Buy worked because it made a direct difference to the households involved by altering their relationship to their dwelling. In other words it was the one policy that actually did put the 'people' first.

Yet of course, this success was achieved by taking the households and dwellings out of social housing: these households were now owner-occupiers and no longer council tenants. We can see some similarities here to the government's *Homes for All* agenda (ODPM, 2005a), which aims to shift the emphasis towards owning rather than renting by using government subsidies and land to support low-cost owner occupation. Might we therefore argue that the government has learnt the lessons of the Right to Buy and is seeking to extend it in this particular policy?

But if this is the case, it poses a dilemma for social housing: can it ever be successful *and* stay socially owned? Are the most successful policies those that are based on the destruction of the sector, or at best a severe restriction of its role and scope of operations? By reform, do we really mean the end of social housing? Much of what follows is an attempt to answer this question. I begin by considering the current policy agenda in more detail in the next two chapters, before outlining a series of proposals which I hope will make clear my answers to these two questions.

5   CURRENT POLICIES

In the last chapter we considered the Right to Buy as an example of a successful housing policy. But another way to view the Right to Buy is as a major intrusion into local autonomy, where central diktat overrode the interests of local social landlords. Assets built and paid for in part from local rates and rents had now to be sold to sitting tenants, with discounts of up to 50 per cent, and furthermore the local authority had to provide a mortgage and so did not often receive much in the way of an immediate capital receipt. Of course, this ignores the purpose of the policy, and it does not mean it was not a success – the policy worked as it was intended to. Nor should we forget those who benefited from what was undoubtedly a popular policy with tenants and the public at large. Yet the Right to Buy was imposed from the top, and as Malpass and Murie (1999) have shown, the implementation of the policy involved a considerable amount of coercion by the Conservative government to ensure that local authorities operated the policy in line with expectations.

Despite the controversy involved in this policy and its effects, however, this imposition of the centre's will is by no means untypical of housing policy of the last 30 years. What this policy did show is that, in Britain's unitary system of government, the centre will also win over the local organisation. Things have developed somewhat since, to the extent that the Labour government is now content to argue that social housing is a national resource which can be adjusted according to national priorities. Hence the Audit Commission (2005) found that local authority tenants in certain parts of the country, such as eastern England, are subsidising tenants in London. The major cultural change in housing over the last 30 years, therefore, has been away from the idea that council housing is a local resource for local people towards the attitude that social housing is a national asset to be determined by national strategies, with local and regional bodies bound by regulation and what has become rather euphemistically known as 'best practice'.

In this chapter I want to consider certain aspects of current housing policy which pertain to social housing. I shall concentrate mainly on policies since 2000. This is not because that year saw any great break in policy – on the contrary, much of the current government's housing policy is an extension of the Conservative agenda developed under both Margaret Thatcher and John Major – but rather because it has led to what might be called a cultural shift regarding the role of social housing.

The key themes

It is my contention that government housing policies can be characterised by three themes. First, as we have already mentioned, the government has centralised the governance of social housing to the extent that it is now perceived as a national asset, with an emphasis placed on the element of national resources used to fund it rather than local resources and objectives. Second, it has expanded social housing provision, but at only limited additional cost to the Exchequer. As we can see in Table 3, planned expend-

Table 3 **Total housing expenditure, 1990–2006**

Year	Actual spending (£ bn)	Real terms*
1990/91	5.8	8.4
1991/92	6.7	9.1
1992/93	6.9	9.1
1993/94	5.8	7.5
1994/95	5.8	7.4
1995/96	5.6	6.9
1996/97	4.9	5.9
1997/98	4.1	4.7
1998/99	4.4	4.9
1999/00	3.7	4.1
2000/01	4.6	5.0
2001/02	5.5	5.8
2002/03	4.9	5.0
2003/04	5.9	5.9
2004/05†	7.3	7.1

* 2003/04 prices using GDP deflator

† Estimated out-turn

Source: Wilcox (2005)

iture as a result of the *Sustainable Communities* plan (2002/03 onwards) is not significantly different from the levels of the 1990s.

What this shows is that the government can only claim a 'step change' in housing expenditure by comparing planned expenditure with the actual expenditure in its first term. Wilcox (2005) shows that if we convert these figures to real terms (at 2003/04 prices) the resources for the Sustainable Communities Plan match expenditure only in the first three years of the 1990s. The current government has used public funds to draw in private finance. In particular, private sector borrowing has been used to fund the expansion in housing association development, as well as the drive to improve the quality of social housing through the use of stock transfer, arm's length management organisations (ALMOs) and the private finance initiative (PFI). The important point here is that government is able to claim the benefits of increased expenditure – or, as it erroneously terms it, 'investment' – without incurring the extra expense itself. This is, of course, a situation that also pertains to its capital programmes in health, education and transport. Third, it has developed policies to deal with differential demand between regions and tenures, and hence growth areas, market renewal areas and use of social housing to expand owner occupation which are part of the *Sustainable Communities* plan and *Homes for All*.

These priorities, particularly the first two, can be seen as extensions of pre-1997 policies. Stock transfer was becoming increasingly significant in the latter years of John Major's government, which also saw the first attempts to use the PFI for housing (King, 2001). Therefore, little has altered in the direction of policy since 1997 other than the scale of activity, in terms of direct government spending and the use of stock transfer and the PFI. I would also suggest that there is little evidence to suggest that much would have changed if a Conservative government had been elected in 2005. What has changed is not so much the direction of policy, but the speed of change towards centralisation and risk aversion by the Treasury.

With regard to the relative significance of these three themes, I would suggest that the dominant theme is that of centralised control. In trying to understand the reasons why it has developed – remembering that it can be dated to the beginning of the Thatcher governments (Jenkins, 1995; King, 2001) – I think we can see it as being part principled and part cultural. One of the principles of the Thatcherite philosophy that dominated government in the

1980s was the need to limit and control the role of intermediate institutions dominated by the professions and trade unions. This was because these bodies were seen as forming a barrier between the state and its subjects (Devigne, 1994). Instead of seeing institutions such as local authorities as playing a positive role in the development of policy, the Conservative governments saw them as one of the causes of Britain's post-war economic and political decline. The Conservatives believed that Britain was becoming ungovernable because of the diverse demands being placed upon the state by groups such as the trade unions, and other institutions. There was perceived to be a breakdown in central authority. Thus a key role for government was to reassert the authority of the state in the face of these competing demands. We can see the effect of this in the public and social policies of the Thatcher governments, which circumscribed the power of the trade unions in the nationalised industries and public sector; they also tried to deal with the professions such as teaching, and constrained the spending and activities of local authorities that could be seen as an alternative source of power.

What is particularly interesting here is that, while the current government's rhetoric may be rather different from that of the Conservatives, it has only sought to fill this space with such unelected bodies as regional housing and planning bodies that have limited local accountability and are heavily dependent on central direction. New Labour may not directly subscribe to the same Conservative principles, but it still finds the situation it inherited in 1997 rather congenial.

The second explanation for centralisation relates to the culture of locating power in the Treasury and seeing this as the legitimate locus of power (Jenkins, 1995). While this developed considerably during the Thatcher and Major administrations, it has reached something of a peak under Gordon Brown's chancellorship, with much of social policy appearing to derive from the Treasury rather than the specific departments of state. Housing policies since the late 1980s, when the government insisted that capital receipts be used to pay off debts and introduced private finance for housing association development (King, 2001), have been determined for the convenience of the Treasury, with strict controls on public spending and limiting of liabilities through risk transfer to the private sector. The effect of this has been to keep significant amounts of borrowing for social housing 'off balance sheet', but without losing control of the assets. This has been achieved by an increase in regulation, with bodies such as the Housing Corporation having a more interventionist approach to housing association governance, despite disbursing fewer funds to a smaller number of associations. The result is a series of hugely complex and bureaucratic mechanisms: so, for example, choice-based lettings have to be imposed and rent targets established rather than rents being determined by demand and landlords being allowed to respond by demolishing unpopular housing and replacing it with better housing or housing in areas of high demand.

So even though the last decade has seen an increasing use of private finance, this has not been a period of liberalisation. Indeed, it is not too far fetched to argue that local housing providers are now almost completely controlled by the centre. This is achieved through a series of policy mechanisms that now largely control the income and expenditure of social landlords, and which determine where new developments will be built and by whom. In the next section I will look at these policies and how they link together.

A master plan?

It is certainly possible to see current policies as being linked by some common purpose. The government suggests that this purpose is to improve the quality of social housing and to allow for greater choice and opportunity in the sector. Accordingly it is attempting to create rent convergence between all social landlords; introduce choice into the lettings process; ensure that local authorities plan for the long term and make effective use of their assets; improve quality by imposing a common standard of amenity; and reform housing benefit. But there is also a different purpose, which is to ensure that government maintains control over social housing and can thereby achieve its objectives without any adverse effects on the public purse, and I believe that we should see these policies in this context.

Of course, it is rather easy to see patterns and suggest that it is all part of some grand plan. In this case, however, the government is quite explicit that these policies are linked, and indeed many of them have developed out of the 2000 Housing Green Paper (DETR, 2000). This does not mean that the policies will succeed in their intentions, but I feel that we should take the government's intentions at face value. So I intend to look at these policies and how they are linked. In doing so I shall analyse their faults and try to assess in what ways they are deficient.

Rent restructuring

This is a national rent-setting policy that largely determines the income of social landlords. It should be seen, among other things, as a form of administrative rent control, in that it sets target rents that social landlords have to achieve by 2012. Indeed, rent restructuring is rather more prescriptive than the statutory controls that were abolished in 1989.

Rent restructuring can be seen as an attempt to restrict rent increases. It also aims, however, to achieve some comparability across all social landlords in a locality. The government argues that 'choice in social housing is distorted when rents differ for no good reason' (ibid.: 5). One of the aims of the policy, therefore, is to 'reduce unjustifiable differences between the rents set by local authorities and by registered social landlords' (ibid.: 93), presumably so that applicants can make informed decisions. Housing association rents in 2000 were on average 20 per cent higher than those of local authorities, and the government felt that there should be some convergence. Moreover, they felt that rents should be set in both sectors according to the same principles, using a formula combining property values and local earnings. Once social housing rents are comparable within a district, applicants, it is argued, will then be able to make comparisons between local social landlords in terms of quality and management, rather than on costs that have arisen as a result of different subsidy systems and rent-setting policies.[1]

But there is a problem here. Information on quality and management is precisely what applicants will lack, unless they have already experienced several local social landlords in the past. Thus the mechanisms determining choice are likely to be reputation and marketing, rather than any accurate assessment of the particular service being offered. What has been expressly removed here is what could act as the main signal to quality, namely price. Rent restructuring makes price competition impossible through

---

[1]   The different subsidy systems, of course, remain.

the bureaucratic imposition of target rents based on common national criteria. Therefore the customer has no ability to make any trade-off between price and quality, but must effectively take both these as given. As a result the criteria used to choose between landlords are likely to be arbitrary and based on stigma and local reputations. This, of course, assumes that local demand conditions allow for any realistic choices in the first place. As we shall see, the choice agenda depends on the availability of options on the supply side, so that an applicant could trade off one offer of accommodation against another. One would have to be particularly ignorant of current supply conditions in many parts of the country to believe that this is actually the case.

So it is very debatable whether rent restructuring will enhance choice in any effective manner. What it does do, however, is give government considerable control over the rent levels and therefore the incomes of social landlords. Indeed, the use of target rents with a cut-off date to achieve convergence means that social landlords now have a particularly clear notion of their income until 2012. This is one side of what can be seen as a pincer effect whereby social landlords are forced down particular routes by the particular mechanisms the government uses to control them.

Decent Homes Standard

The other side of the pincer, which affects the expenditure side, is the Decent Homes Standard. Like rent restructuring, this is a policy that affects the behaviour of social landlords in the long term by channelling their priorities towards stock improvement above all other areas of activity. In effect the prescriptions laid down by the Decent Homes Standard inform social landlords of their obligations in terms of dwelling standards and quantify the cost of improvements needed to attain this standard. To meet the Decent Homes Standard each dwelling must:

- meet the current statutory minimum standard for housing;
- be in a reasonable state of repair;
- have reasonably modern facilities and services (bathroom, kitchen, etc.);
- provide a reasonable degree of thermal comfort (efficient heating and effective insulation).

In many ways this is the key component in the government's strategy for social housing, in that achieving the standard by 2010 drives the decision-making of social landlords. The starting point of the policy is for landlords to inspect and value their stock (something that local authorities had already undertaken as part of resource accounting; see below). As a result landlords are now able to apply a benchmark to their stock, in terms of current valuation and survey data, and to relate this to the government's expectations of what standards ought to be. They are therefore able to cost the remedial action needed to meet the standard.

The Decent Homes Standard, taken together with rent restructuring, means that the government now exercises considerable control over the activities of social landlords and is able to determine both income and expenditure. But there is a further policy, specific to local authorities, which exerts yet more pressure.

Resource accounting and business planning

This policy actually pre-dates the two already discussed, having been proposed in 1998 and introduced in 2001. Resource accounting can be seen as attempting several things. First, it recognises officially what had long since been the reality, that the role of local authorities has now changed to that of managers and maintainers rather than developers of housing. Resource accounting recognised this by shifting the emphasis away from historic debt incurred in asset formation (the cost of house building) to a form of accounting that records the current value of assets. This means that each authority has to be aware of the condition of its housing stock and the amount of money needed to improve it. Resource accounting can be seen as an attempt to 'measure on a consistent basis the resources used over the lifetime of houses, rather than simply the cash spent on them each year' (Malpass and Aughton, 1999: 34).

The government intends resource accounting to make local authorities more businesslike in their operation and to encourage them to manage their assets more effectively. Accordingly, they are now expected to submit annual business plans for their housing revenue account.[2] These plans will indicate how the authority intends to use and enhance its assets over a period of up to 30 years. Indeed, the political aim of business planning is to ensure that local authorities are clear about the nature and scale of the problems facing them and what options are available to them. It forces local authorities to concentrate on long-term planning and the need to maintain and improve their own stock.

It is this need for long-term planning which is the really significant part of this housing revenue framework, and this becomes clear when we link it to the previous two policies. The limitations

---

2   This is the account that deals with all income and expenditure on the authority's own housing stock.

of rent restructuring mean that local authorities know what income they have at their disposal until 2012. The Decent Homes Standard informs them what they must do to improve their assets by 2010. There is therefore no opportunity for ignorance on the part of landlords about the scale of the problems facing them. For many local authorities this means a deficit between their projected income and their necessary expenditure. They are therefore forced to consider means of addressing this shortfall, and for this the government has given them three options: stock transfer, establishing an arm's length management organisation, or the private finance initiative. All these measures involve the use of private finance.

Private finance

Housing policy since the late 1980s has depended on private finance in order to meet successive governments' aims. This was begun in 1989 under the Conservatives, who allowed housing association funding to pre-determined grant rates to be topped up with private borrowing. At the same time many local authorities began to transfer their entire stock to newly formed housing associations as a means of circumventing government restrictions on the use of their capital receipts. This too used private finance to purchase the dwellings and to improve them. Between 1988 and 2003 there was an injection of £26 billion of private finance into social housing, in addition to government expenditure on housing associations in this period of £24 billion (Wilcox, 2005). Private finance has therefore allowed for a doubling of housing association activity over and above what it would have been if it had relied solely on government subsidies. So, the first reason for this policy is that it has allowed for an expansion of activity without huge costs to the Treasury. Private borrowing by housing associations does not count as public borrowing, and thus does not add to the public debt. We can see why the transfer of council housing to housing associations has such an appeal.

But there is also a more positive reason often given for the use of private finance. Borrowing from commercial lenders would ensure greater value for money and efficiency in social housing. Social landlords would have to be more cost conscious and businesslike in their approach. They would be encouraged to plan more for the long term because they would now be committed to long-term debt financing. The Conservatives, but also many within New Labour, earnestly believed in private sector solutions to deal with social problems. It was believed that disciplines from private business would be an improvement on public bureaucracies. The language of the former Conservative government has been moderated somewhat by Labour – they are now more likely to talk of 'social entrepreneurialism' – but the essential elements of policy have remained and have even been developed. What has altered since 2000 is the scale of the use of private finance and the emphasis placed on stock transfer as a key vehicle to meet government policy objectives. The Conservatives operated a quota limiting stock transfer to 25,000 properties per annum for much of the 1990s. The 2000 Housing Green Paper increased this to a target of 200,000 per year.

Stock transfer is clearly the government's preferred option for social housing. The effects of business planning, and the control of income and expenditure, have exerted pressure on local authorities to make fundamental decisions in the knowledge that most will not receive sufficient resources to meet the Decent Homes

Standard by 2010. The effect is that much of the cost of stock improvements is funded privately, but without any diminution of government regulation.

There are, however, two alternatives to stock transfer open to local authorities. High-performing local authorities – i.e. those meeting most of the government's performance indicators – can seek to establish an ALMO. This is where a separate management company is set up to manage and improve the housing stock. Additional funding is available from government for ALMOs, and as with stock transfer, an ALMO needs to be approved by tenants and (also as with stock transfer) is subject to a bidding procedure and needs the sanction of the secretary of state.

Another alternative to stock transfer, which avoids losing political control, is the PFI. The PFI began in the mid-1990s as a means of using private sector finance and expertise in the public sector. It is a means of transferring risk from the Treasury to the private sector by undertaking large capital projects 'off balance sheet'. This means that these capital projects do not appear as public borrowing. A PFI is funded through revenue over a 30-year period, for which government credits are available, instead of the traditional system of capital funding whereby the full cost would fall completely on the Treasury. So the PFI does not involve up-front borrowing and thus large-scale projects can be funded, with the current generation of politicians taking the credit, but without any effect on immediate government spending and borrowing. A PFI needs government approval, and this has added to their complexity, with both the Treasury and the private service provider seeking to ensure that they are insulated from risk. As a result a large PFI scheme in Camden was halted by the ODPM in 2005 on the grounds that it carried too much risk and did not represent sufficient value for money. Importantly, there-fore, a PFI still needs central government approval before it can go ahead. The PFI is perhaps most applicable when tenants refuse to sanction a transfer, or where the local authority wishes to retain ownership but cannot meet the required performance standards.

There has been a lot of debate about whether these three options are sufficient to allow all local authorities to meet the Decent Homes Standard. For example, Birmingham City Council (the biggest housing authority in England) has failed to secure the right result in a tenants' ballot, is poorly rated and cannot use the PFI because the scale of disrepair of housing stock would be prohibitive for a private investor. Local authorities such as this therefore currently have no viable options to meet the demands placed on them by government. The government has, however, ruled out any 'fourth option' for local authorities and is not prepared to relax the requirements of the Decent Homes Standard. It argues that no other option is necessary, but, in reality, the reason it has ruled out alternative policy options has more to do with practical politics. Any 'fourth option' allowing local authorities extra funding and/or borrowing while retaining their stock would quickly become the option of choice among many local authorities, as well as causing a huge uproar among those authorities that had already used one of the three current options. I believe that a 'fourth option' will eventually have to be offered, but the government will seek to delay this until such time as only the 'basket case' authorities remain.

The effect of the use of private finance has been, and will be, significant. But policy since 1989 is actually based on something of a myth. Successive governments have argued that using private finance has introduced commercial disciplines. Social landlords, it is said, need to operate as businesses rather than as welfare bodies. They have to ensure that they can meet their liabilities and manage their assets. But social landlords are still very far from being fully risk-bearing businesses. Social landlords still hold a monopoly over local provision, and as associations merge and local authorities transfer their stock, the number of local providers diminishes and the level of local influence they have increases. In addition to this, the level of regulation by government and its agencies, such as the Housing Corporation, has been extended greatly under the cloak of apparent privatisation. Housing associations are not free to dispose of their assets, increase (or decrease) their rents, or even determine whom they house. Most housing associations are still dependent on central government funding, and thus must accept this detailed and prescriptive regulation. Yet instead of being under democratic control, they are accountable only to themselves and the government agencies that fund them. Associations, as we have seen in Chapter 1, make much of how they are community based, but there is no formality to this. In fact housing associations are managed by self-selecting groups, advised by consultants from the same cultural milieu (and who are often former senior employees of social landlords), whose policies are driven by the government's priorities and enacted through Housing Corporation regulation and funding priorities. Their basis in the community is merely a rhetorical trope based on the necessity of conforming to the government's expectations.

The net effect of this combination of private finance and centralised control has not led to any liberalisation: there is little or no competition between providers, and little opportunity for innovation and variety without government sanction. Instead of liberalisation, what we have is a situation of greater dependence on government and an emphasis on central control. In addition, what has been consistently eroded is any sense of democratic control of housing assets and any local political accountability. Accountability is upwards, towards regional and national bodies established by government, and no longer to the local community. Ironically this is completely at odds with the recent rhetoric of social landlords with their emphasis on being community-oriented businesses (NHF, 2003).

Sustainable Communities plan

The third key theme is the most current, namely that of dealing with differential demand. Superficially, this might seem to be a different sort of policy from those we have just considered. As I have already suggested, the *Sustainable Communities* plan is concerned with developing growth areas of new housing development in the South, where the demand for housing and house prices are both high and rising, and the regeneration of abandoned and low-demand housing areas, involving mass demolition, in areas of the North and the Midlands. The common theme of these two approaches of growth and renewal is the idea of 'building' communities, be it from scratch or by reinvigorating depressed areas. The result is that the bulk of new housing investment is being targeted at these areas, with the effect that being included in a growth area or a housing market renewal pathfinder has considerable consequences for local housing organisations. Moreover, the shift to large-scale and volume development favours large regional or national housing associations and has led to a rush by associations to join housing consortia or merge to form a larger body capable of competing successfully for volume building.

What ought to be readily apparent is that the *Sustainable Communities* plan is consistent with the centralisation of policy already identified. The growth areas and pathfinders are determined by government, which controls the agenda and establishes the rules for development. Hence the significance of the ODPM's insistence that 60 per cent of new development should employ 'innovative' building techniques rather than allowing social landlords to develop in the manner they see fit. More than any other, this policy shows that social housing has been 'nationalised', so that government feels that it can determine the allocation of resources and target them as it sees fit.

This has an important consequence in that housing policy has shifted from being uniform and consistent across the country (albeit with diversity of tenure patterns, rents and access opportunities) to being national, in a different way: it is no longer consistent across the country, but it is directed from the centre to meet particular targets and aims based on national strategies. Social housing policy is no longer about ensuring a consistent coverage of housing, but is instead about chasing notions of 'demand' rather than 'need'. This idea of demand is not, however, based on local market signals, but on the assumptions of the planning system and the imposition of central house building targets, based, as the Barker Report (HM Treasury, 2004) commented, on out-of-date demographics. The result is the imposition of housing in certain areas regardless of the wishes of the local community, alongside the compulsory purchase and demolition of dwellings in other areas as they are deemed superfluous and if they are apparently not compatible with the government's notion of 'community'. As a result many actually existing communities in the north of England are blighted by the threat of compulsory purchase and demolition, leading to a self-justifying atrophy. Indeed, the establishment of housing market renewal pathfinders in certain areas such as Hull (John Prescott's constituency) has led to increasing house prices as property speculators buy up derelict properties in the knowledge that they will be compulsorily purchased for considerably more than was paid for them.

The *Sustainable Communities* plan can therefore be seen as a rather incoherent attempt to impose a model of diversity devised by the centre on localities that have no recourse but to accept it. Likewise, social landlords, entirely dependent on government funding and cowed by regulation, have no alternative but to join in this spurious game of 'building communities'.

Homes for All

The most recent initiative from the Blair government, announced in early 2005, might be seen as the first public recognition by government that social housing has become superfluous. This policy involves the introduction of a First Time Buyer Initiative which allows 15,000 low-income households and key workers to buy an equity share in a dwelling (many of these new dwellings will be built on publicly owned land); a competition for developers to bid to provide houses at a price of £60,000, again using public land; and an initiative called HomeBuy for social housing tenants to enable them to buy, at a discount, an equity share in their dwelling of between 50 and 100 per cent. The government suggests that this will make ownership affordable for around 300,000 tenants.

Of course, the dominance of owner occupation is by no means new, nor is the preparedness of government to use social housing to further owner occupation, as we have seen in our discussion of the Right to Buy. What is different, however, with the Homes for All agenda is that the proclaimed justification – owner occupation for all – was not so much that of independence or even choice, but social justice. The government's argument was that low-income households deserved access to owner occupation just like the more affluent who already had ready access. Traditionally, of course, social housing was justified on the basis of social justice, and this was the case as recently as the Borrie Commission (1995; and see Brown, 1999). The view of government, however, is now to divert resources away from social housing and towards owner occupation *in the name of social justice*. Of course, we may see a more cynical motive in this policy, which appears to prioritise households for subsidy based on the electoral significance of the part of the public sector they are employed in.

It is hard as yet to gauge the full significance of these last two policies. I have identified how they both continue long-standing policies and develop social housing in new areas. It may well be that these policies, added to the increased use of private finance, actually present a fundamental challenge to social housing to the extent that we begin to question whether it still retains any purpose. This is an issue to which I return in Chapter 6.

Choice

One of the issues I have not yet dealt with, and indeed not identified as a key theme, is that of choice. This is not because it is insignificant or has not been part of the government's policies. Indeed, like the use of private finance and centralisation, the emphasis on choice pre-dates 1997 and has been an important part of housing policy, particularly in terms of the promotion of owner occupation. It is my view, however, that choice-based policies, whatever the rhetoric, are subservient to the main focus of centralised control. As an example, the government announced 'targets' for choice-based lettings in April 2002, which required that 25 per cent of local authorities should have such a system by 2005, and 100 per cent by 2010 (Brown et al., 2002). This statement was made during the life of the 27 pilot schemes established to look at the viability of various plans, and prior to the large-scale evaluation exercise of these pilots which was not published until 2004 (Marsh et al., 2004). This suggests that the policy of choice-based lettings is a 'top-down' initiative that seeks to impose a particular agenda on social landlords, tenants and applicants.

Choice is being promoted by the government, but households and housing providers are being offered choice only on the government's terms. Proposals such as resource accounting and stock transfer might have the proclaimed aim of enhancing local autonomy. But the government is always there to tell housing organisations what they should do with their autonomy. More generally, in the emerging public policy literature on central–local relations in the UK, the phrase 'earned autonomy' is gaining ground (Pratchett, 2002). This emphasises the fact that the current government's priorities are clearly articulated and understood by local authorities and housing associations, and will be driven through by a mixture of 'carrot and stick' incentives and regulations. Autonomy will be earned through meeting performance targets but will still be heavily circumscribed.

But then one can question whether these policies really have anything particularly to do with empowerment and individual decision-making (Brown and King, 2005). Instead current choice-based policies seem more aimed at controlling supply-side activity, i.e. concerned with what landlords are doing and the quality and quantity of their provision. Choice-based letting does not alter the demand side, in that choice is still controlled and rationed by the landlord rather than by the purported decision-maker (the tenant or applicant). This system does not alter the supply of housing, nor does it change the conditions for accessing housing, in that 'need', as determined by the landlord using government's 'best practice', still forms the main criterion for accessing the housing register.

This misuse of choice can also be seen in the area of housing benefit reform. In the name of individual empowerment, the government seeks to reform the housing benefit system so that all payments are made to tenants, who therefore become responsible for their rent payments. In addition, instead of tenants receiving their full rent they will get a local housing allowance which will allow them to 'shop around' (DWP, 2002). There is much merit in this policy, as I have argued elsewhere (King, 1999, 2000). What is missing from government policy here, and why one fears the reforms will fail, is that very little thought has been given to the effects of changing the manner in which housing benefit is paid. In particular, there is no attempt to advise, guide or train tenants with no history of paying their rent. This is a hugely important point, in that over 70 per cent of social housing tenants currently have their rent paid directly to the landlord. Ensuring that tenants respond properly to these changes will need considerable management, as is shown by a voluntary pilot by London and Quadrant Housing Association, which found that, within six months of allowing their tenants to receive payments, arrears had risen by 300 per cent. This leads to the suggestion that the main impact and effect of the housing benefit reforms will be on landlord behaviour, especially in the private rented sector, where landlords can choose to let to groups other than benefit claimants.

In the social sector, if these reforms were to be implemented,[3] it would cause a considerable reorientation of the housing service, with a shift back to basic activities, such as rent collection and arrears recovery, as well as altering the relations between landlord and tenant. These changes are all to be welcomed, in that a shift away from areas that social landlords are not good at dealing with, and which are often at the expense of management and maintenance, is eminently sensible and long overdue. My concern here is that the manner in which the housing benefit reforms are being introduced may cause hardship for tenants, who might get into arrears, and for landlords, who might get into financial difficulties and who have no enhanced remedies to support them. The changes seem more designed to impact on organisations, and the effects on individuals have not been fully considered. This is noticeable in that the evaluation of the reforms so far has concentrated on the administration of the system rather than on the behaviour of landlords and tenants.

In Chapter 7 I shall discuss the need for a return to the 'basics' of housing management and how real choice-based policies can be implemented. My view is that we should build on the reforms to housing benefit, but for them to be effective they need to be managed and the nature of the functions of landlords needs to be questioned. But before considering any proposals for reform I want to look at a related aspect of recent housing policy. As we

---

3   The reforms are currently at the pathfinder stage and apply only to the private sector. They are expected to be implemented nationally by 2008 and extended to the social sector once rent restructuring has been completed in 2012.

have seen in this chapter, policy is concerned with such abstractions as 'decent', 'choice', 'sustainable' and 'community'. It is no longer enough for social housing to be concerned with maintenance, management or regeneration. It is as if the government has to describe housing policy in new ways in order to signal its distinctiveness. Whether giving something a fancy name actually makes it different, however, is certainly open to question.

6 ALL TALK – THE CHANGING CULTURE OF HOUSING

In this chapter I want to take a step back from looking at policy mechanisms and look at the labels that the government has put on them. Since 1997 there has been a new jargon of social housing, which has seen the appropriation of such terms as 'home', 'decent', 'together', 'community' and 'supporting people' to create a particular image or identity for social housing. We have seen the use of certain rather abstract words and phrases, which often do not have a precise meaning, but which are seen as 'virtuous concepts'. These have been turned into technical terms with a specific meaning somewhat at odds with their traditional definition. We can think of words such as 'home' instead of 'house' or 'dwelling unit', 'decent' instead of 'habitable' or 'good quality', and the phrase 'sustainable communities' as the specific aim of policy.

Some might argue that this is merely a semantic argument, and that what matters is not what policies are called but whether they succeed. In answer to this we should ask how can we measure something we cannot define. More fundamentally, however, there is a suspicion that the renaming of policies and practices is essentially a displacement activity aimed at giving the impression of newness and fresh thinking, when in fact, as we have seen, current policy is actually more a continuation of policies developed in the 1980s and 1990s. Of course, this is not restricted to housing but has become general, so that government never 'spends' but 'invests'; policies are never 'introduced' but 'rolled out'; and we never look to the future, being too busy 'going forward'. The government wants us to believe that things have changed because they have been renamed, and it seems to have concentrated on this rather than actually thinking about what it is spending money on, how policies are implemented, and planning for the future. As we saw in the previous chapter, what has been described as a 'step change' really means nothing more than returning to the spending levels at the time John Major became prime minister. It is also worth noting that the phrases used to describe policy are general aims with which no reasonable person can disagree – this makes it more difficult to focus opposition to specific policies. For example, who is opposed to 'sustainable communities', or proposes fostering 'unsustainable communities'?

We can get a sense of these tactics by looking at the very idea of a 'sustainable community'. It appears initially to show some ambition – the creation of new and vibrant communities that have all the necessary linkages and facilities – but in fact shows a rather confused and naive sense of what its achievement might actually mean. At the root of the problem is an inability to actually define what a 'sustainable community' is. In the government's key policy document (ODPM, 2003) there is no definition of the term, merely a series of twelve bullet points outlining the 'requirements' for a sustainable community. These points purport to tell us what makes a community sustainable, but they do not tell us what a community might be, or what it is to be sustainable. It seems to be assumed that we all already know what a community is, and the document uses the term as if there is no controversy about its usage. Instead the twelve bullet points are full of abstractions such as 'flourishing', 'strong', 'effective', 'sufficient', 'good', and so on. All these terms are unquantifiable and question-begging, in that we are not told what it means to flourish, or how we might measure it, nor what 'effective', 'sufficient' or 'good' actually might mean. These abstract terms are all eminently laudable and describe things we would hope to achieve, but they are also vague and do not relate to anything definitive, or to any situation where we can categorically claim success or failure. The main argument behind 'sustainable communities', as we have seen, is that 'housing is not enough' and that there needs to be a supportive infrastructure. This, of course, is hardly a revelation to anyone involved in housing and planning, or indeed anyone who has ever walked to the shops or waited at a bus stop. The need for infrastructure is a commonplace in any housing or planning textbook and in most government policy-making since the shift towards renovation and regeneration in the late 1960s.

In trying to come to a practical definition of a 'sustainable community' we must conclude that it boils down to *that which is deserving of government subsidy*. The term merely describes a targeted subsidy mechanism aimed at altering certain supply conditions in areas of high and low demand, creating growth and regeneration areas to meet demographic assumptions determined centrally. The term now merely has a technical meaning for a specific government policy, such that neither 'sustainable' nor 'community' could now be used in any different context.

This is by no means the sole example of taking ordinary words and phrases and turning them into technical terms with a specific meaning. Government appears to consider that giving its policies and institutions what might be called soft and inclusive terms somehow alters the tenor of the policy. In terms of current policy we can point to the mechanism funding provision for the elderly and those with special needs banally called 'Supporting People'; the policy aimed at improving housing standards in the social sector, which we have discussed already in the last chapter, namely the Decent Homes Standard (with the consequence that a house now becomes 'decent' only if it fulfils national criteria relating to such things as the age of kitchen units and boiler, and thermal insulation); and, third, the campaign against anti-social behaviour organised by the Home Office called 'Together'. All these policies expropriate general expressions that can now only be used in a specific sense that empties them of any other meaning. It is now the case that a house is 'decent' because of a national standard, regardless of the views of the landlord or the person living in it. More generally, a term that has connotations of politeness, respectability and conventionality is now reduced merely to a technical term for a minimum standard. One can see the need for quality housing and the imposition of standards, but without this decline into banality.

I would argue that the reason for this use of banality is precisely because policy-makers are aware of the disconnection between their policies and the manner in which housing is used. Notions of decency, togetherness and support have a natural resonance with the manner in which we live in dwelling environments and communities, and so it is hoped to gain by connecting functional policies to these terms. There is, however, no change in the nature of policy-making, in that these policies are national standards, assessed through top-down target-setting and sanctions. All these policies have is a rather gentler, if less meaningful, name (does 'Together' actually tell the uninitiated anything about what it is?), but they are no nearer to connecting with the manner in which we use our housing.

Perhaps the most glaring example of the inappropriate use of an abstract term is the now almost ubiquitous use of the term 'homes' to refer to brick boxes built by social landlords and private developers (King, 2004). There is an apparent belief that calling dwellings 'homes' connects more with the eventual users. Accordingly, housing and building professions, as well as politicians, now commonly use 'home' instead of 'house' when they refer to physical structures, and social landlords manage and build 'homes' and not 'dwellings' or 'houses'.

All this does, however, is devalue the concept of home and denude it of any serious meaning. 'Home' just becomes another technical term, like 'dwelling unit', used by professionals. The reason for this is clearly that 'home' is a warmer, more emotive concept, which converts a brick box into something with a much stronger resonance. Accordingly, when we discuss those lacking a dwelling, we call them 'homeless' to emphasise the full import of what they are suffering, and the full possibility of its redemption. 'House' is a colder word which becomes inhabited and warm when translated into 'home'.

Speaking only of homes adds a greater significance to what housing professionals are doing: they are not building or managing brick boxes, but creating something warm and welcoming to residents. The misuse is significant in that it implies that homes are 'made' by those other than the household. Homes, we are now led to believe, are fashioned by professionals ready-made for people to live in. This situation has several consequences. First, because a home is ostensibly created by professionals, this implies that no effort is needed on the part of the household. The suggestion is that homemaking is easy to achieve and can be readily done *for us*. Second, this view carries the apparent belief that a home is transient. Building homes implies that we move from one home to another and do not take *our home* with us. A home is made for us to move into and we should be grateful. Third, this idea implies the standardisation of homes according to professionals' understanding of their clients' needs and aspirations. The result is the provision of identikit homes, based on standard design briefs and models. This creates an increasing homogeneity of styles aimed to fulfil standardised purposes. We need only think of terms such as 'starter home' and 'executive home' to see this process of standardisation. Fourth, this will tend to impersonalise the notion of home and dwelling more generally: it becomes a commodity that is bought and sold rather than a place of intimacy and nurturing. Housing is commodified according to economic rather than human values (King, 1996; Turner, 1976). Lastly, but implicit in all the above, this notion of home assumes the professionalisation of the role of homemaking: homes can be made only by others, by 'the experts'. Professionals tell us what we need or, in other words, they actually dare to tell us what home is.

But the appropriation of these terms does not mean that anything changes. Instead we can see that these terms might actually mask the fact that little is actually meant to change, and that the hyperbole of current housing policy detracts from the fact that we have seen only rather timid and managerial changes. These are only continuations or extensions of pre-1997 policies aimed at keeping the centre in control of the policy agenda. Spending has not increased in the dramatic fashion the government claims; the policies do not have the reach that they claim; and what is occurring is often a result of tinkering and not fundamental reform. What is certainly not there is any real attempt to implement real choice in housing for those who currently do not enjoy it.

7   A BLUEPRINT FOR CHANGE

Introduction

We can agree with some parts of what the government seeks to achieve, particularly extending choice. But, as should now be obvious, there is much about its policies that is deeply problematical. There are difficulties both in terms of policies and in the general approach, which is actually inimical to a choice-based agenda and will be counter-productive, and can be seen, at best, as naive and ill thought out or, at worst, as disingenuous and cynical.

The heart of the government's failure is that it will not allow policy and practice to develop organically. It has nationalised policy-making and has sought a monopoly over decision-making. It does not appear to trust social landlords to develop their own policies and respond to local conditions as they see fit. As a result social landlords are increasingly dependent on government for both funding and direction – even though we have seen an increase in the use of private finance – and tenants and applicants are no more empowered than they ever were. As we have suggested, the only housing policy that has succeeded in empowering individuals has been the Right to Buy, which gave households direct control over an asset. By way of contrast, current policies place no power in the hands of tenants, but rather are oriented towards setting targets and performance indicators for social landlords to achieve within a national policy framework. Politicians may claim that these policies are about empowerment, but they are aimed at doing things on behalf of people on the assumption that politicians know best.

Current policies are concerned with controlling resources and activity to ensure that the Treasury is not exposed. This is masked by an increasingly hyperbolic rhetoric aimed at suggesting that the policy agenda is new and distinctive. Yet these policies are actually continuations of policies from the 1980s and 1990s. There has been precious little original thinking about housing in recent years, and certainly nothing to match the reforms initiated by the Conservatives in 1980 and 1988/89. Plans for reforms since 1997 have sought to build on the policies of the Conservatives, extending stock transfer, the use of private finance and an attenuated form of choice. Of course, this has meant a lot of activity and new initiatives for social landlords to deal with, having to introduce rent restructuring, choice-based lettings, Supporting People, and so on. But these are meant primarily to push forward the same agenda. Indeed, where there is a difference in the current government's housing policy agenda, it is largely in terms of an increased complexity and bureaucratisation of the policy process, and a use of overblown rhetoric to disguise managerialism.

The proposals I outline in this chapter are aimed at offering a concrete alternative to these housing policies. Certain of the proposals will be apparently based on the same principles, particularly choice. As we have seen, however, much of the choice agenda is illusory, and so instead I seek to suggest means of introducing real choice. The way to achieve this is by reforming the supply side of the housing market and by distinguishing between types of renting. The aim here is to encourage genuine competition between landlords, not as under the current regime whereby social landlords compete for government funding, but through real competition at the local level, whereby landlords have to respond to the wants and needs of local people. This would involve a radical shift in decision-making back to the level of individual organisations and households and away from national performance targets.

A key to any reform is to question just what the role of a landlord is. It is my view that landlords need to return to basics, and concentrate on their core activities. They should forget notions of being 'in business' for anybody but themselves and their immediate tenants, and leave the development of sustainability to communities themselves. Social landlords have considerable expertise, but this relates to the managing and maintaining of dwellings, and this is what they need to focus on.

The key to any subsidy system should be the particular circumstances of a household and the ability of its members to find housing for themselves. This means we should question seriously who is being subsidised, and why. In particular, we may want to encourage owner occupation for the benefits it brings to households, but why should we subsidise it with public funds and assets? As regards rented housing, we need to break down the division between social and private landlords through a common tenancy for all rented housing, and move towards a subsidy system that is focused on the needs of individuals rather than landlords. We should aim to achieve a housing system that is largely neutral in terms of whom it assists. Moreover, the emphasis of any subsidy system should never be judged in terms of its effects on landlords, but only on what it can do for individual households.

I would suggest that there are only two grounds for subsidies: first, for those households where lack of income prevents them from gaining access to good-quality housing; and second, where individuals are vulnerable or incapable owing to disability or infirmity.

The importance of these supply-side reforms is to allow for proper and effective choice at the level of individual households. For choice to work there need to be real alternatives, and this can be achieved only by competition between landlords. But choice also means that resources have to be available to individual households. Hence I suggest that subsidies be shifted entirely over to the demand side and paid directly to individuals. Direct payments are, of course, part of current policy, but, as I have discussed in Chapter 5, this needs to be backed up with a proper support structure. Instead of being concerned with strategies and community development, the emphasis of the housing profession needs to shift to individualised support structures to assist only vulnerable households and ensure that they become able to manage their own resources. Choice, after two generations of state dependency, cannot necessarily be implemented without some systems of temporary support.

These are the principles and the basic outline of what I propose is needed to reform rented housing (see Box 2). In the rest of this chapter I provide a more detailed discussion and justification for them. My aim is very much geared towards putting forward a positive programme, rather than concentrating on the particular means for achieving it. In particular, it is not my intention to dwell on the cost of these proposals. This is because my aim is not particularly to save money compared with the current fiscal cost of supporting housing policy. My aim is to provide a framework

---

> **Box 2 Making choice work**
> Three principles for proper choice
>
> - competition between landlords
> - demand-side subsidies
> - supporting the choosers

for policy that will ensure the best use of any money that is spent, by offering a realistic degree of choice.

A future for social housing?

The first issue I want to deal with is the fundamental one of whether there is still any role for social housing at all. The emphasis in housing policies, as we have seen, has been the attempted commercialisation of the social sector through the use of private finance and the encouragement of choice. But this is still within the constraints of national policy. Efficiency is encouraged not through competition or by exposure to the needs and demands of customers, but through central regulation. Moreover, current policies do not alter the monopoly position of landlords as the sole providers of one type of housing, and this is a real obstacle to choice and diversity. This problem is becoming increasingly significant in the current climate of stock transfer, and partnerships or mergers between social landlords. We will soon have a situation where one large housing association – normally arising as a result of stock transfer – dominates in an area, and where a small number of large regional and national housing groups dominate new development and take the majority of funding. So despite the rhetoric of diversity and the talk of new management and delivery vehicles, we are entering a period of greater homogeneity and a reduction in diversity. This is backed up by a standardising regulatory framework, which uses the notion of 'best practice' to enforce a common set of policies and operating procedures across all social landlords.

In contrast to this I believe reforms are needed that break the monopoly of one sort of landlord and create proper diversity and competition. The way to achieve this is not to regulate existing organisations. This would merely enhance the current trend towards the nationalisation of social housing. Rather we should question why we need any distinctions between landlords at all. Do we still need organisations with the label 'social', if they are being encouraged to act commercially, to compete and to provide both rented and owner-occupied housing? What is so special about the label that needs preservation at a time when there is a consensus on the virtues of choice and responsibility? Indeed, what meaning is there to the idea of social housing if the emphasis is now on enhancing opportunities for ownership? The logic of government policy is therefore to shift away from social housing as a safety net for the vulnerable. It is ceasing to have a specific welfare function. This is something that ought to be extended, with the aim of ridding rented housing of the artificial divisions that create stigma and discriminate against those unable to access social housing.

What is needed therefore is the ending of the privileged status of social landlords in terms of receipt of subsidies, tax concessions and statutory protection so that there is no longer any distinction between landlords in rented housing. The process of stock transfer needs to be accelerated and become compulsory, so that all rented housing is in the hands of private bodies. Where necessary, particularly in large urban areas, the break-up of the stock and its disbursement either to existing landlords or to a number of new private bodies specifically created for the purpose should be encouraged. There would be no need to alter the current legal status of housing associations, except in a liberalising manner to allow them to use their surpluses in any manner they determine.

The vexed issue here, as currently with stock transfer procedures, is the need to hold a successful ballot of tenants before any change in ownership of the stock. Since 1986 successive reforms have included the need to secure the consent of tenants, and attempts to introduce reforms without a tenant ballot, such as Housing Action Trusts as part of the Housing Act 1988, had to be altered before the legislation was enacted. Nonetheless there are problems with ballots, particularly because of the fact that they are binding on those who voted against the transfer and on future tenants. So, for instance, a local authority might secure a comfortable 75/25 outcome in favour of transfer and therefore go ahead. But with a turnover of new tenants of only 5 per cent per annum it might well be that any majority for transfer could theoretically disappear within six years. The main justification for balloting tenants, however, was that they were faced with a monopoly provider and they had no alternative form of accommodation other than their current landlord. But the reforms I am suggesting would create proper competition between landlords and thus households would have alternatives. This would mean that households would not merely have the one-off choice of a new landlord (though, of course, with the same staff and policies), but could choose between a number of landlords. This would not offer a perfect choice, nor would it guarantee that everyone would get what they wanted. But perfection is unachievable and should never be the aim of choice-based policies. What should be the guide for success, as I discussed in Chapter 4, is the ability that a household has to control its own dwelling – its own private space, not some nebulous community or neighbourhood – and the reduction of the power of landlords through competition would go a long way to achieving this. What empowers a household is not a one-off choice over which landlord they pay their rent to, but whether they can control their immediate environment and use it in a manner that allows them the greatest opportunity to fulfil their own ends. Therefore I believe that it is justifiable to abolish the need for tenants' ballots and allow landlords to determine the use of their assets as they see fit, within the normal bounds of law.

An essential part of this change would be the creation of a common legal structure for tenancy for all rented housing, so that all tenants have the same rights, and landlords can offer their dwellings on the same basis. This is an issue that has arisen from time to time and is generally seen as being something to be desired. The problem, however, is how to create this in a manner that is acceptable both to current private landlords and social housing tenants. The extension of assured shorthold tenancies to all rented housing would mean a significant reduction in tenants' rights, while assured tenancies of unrestricted length would not be welcomed by private landlords, at least not without increased powers of eviction. If one had to choose between the two possibilities, however, it is the latter that we should prefer. But to balance this we should also give landlords an enhanced right to possession in cases of rent arrears and abuse of the property. The proposals regarding shifting subsidies to the demand side, discussed in the next section, will also necessitate this strengthening of landlords' rights.

Part of any such denationalisation of housing would be the demolition of the system of regulation that currently controls social landlords. Policy and the requisite resources need to be localised so that decisions relating to rent levels, new building and demolitions and so on are determined by individual landlords. All this can and should be managed within a local framework of planning and building guidelines that ensure quality and standards. But regulation should relate to building and planning issues only, with key decisions taken locally. In particular, the level of house building is not a matter for central government. Much of housing and planning policy appears to be aimed at keeping house prices artificially high, rather than actually enhancing affordability and sustainability, as is often claimed. We can see this in the new planning directive released for consultation in July 2005 (ODPM, 2005b). The aim of this change is to require local planners to release land in response to increases in house prices. As Ferdinand Mount has stated, this is precisely the tactic used by De Beers to keep the price of diamonds artificially high (*Daily Telegraph*, 20 July 2005, p. 28). Incredibly, the government appears to actually believe that this will assist affordability rather than just maintain house prices at their already high levels. But this is just another consequence of trying to determine housing outcomes through national targets.

Localising decision-making would mean that there would be no need to retain the unaccountable structures of regional housing and planning boards and the Housing Corporation. These bodies exist to meet the requirements of central government and would have no place in a properly private system based on competition between landlords. As I discuss below, shifting subsidies to the demand side would also mean that these bodies would be largely redundant and could be abolished with no great impact.

What these changes would achieve, therefore, would be the effective end of social housing as a distinct sector (see Box 3). Instead there would just be landlords offering rented housing without any distinction in their legal status. The aim of any subsidy system should be supporting households rather than a particular type of landlord. As Oxley and Smith (1996) have argued, we should not be so concerned with who owns the dwellings as who lives in them. This, after all, is how many countries in Europe and states in the USA operate their subsidy systems. Indeed, it is a peculiarity of housing in Britain that we are so concerned about ownership rather than who is being helped. This leads to the unfortunate assumption that whoever is housed in social housing is deserving of it and that a dwelling should be subsidised merely because a particular type of organisation has built it. We can see this in current policy, where building dwellings to sell to public sector professionals is deemed to be a proper use of public subsidy (ODPM, 2005a).

Where landlords would be distinguishable would be in the types of property they were prepared to let and to whom, the areas where they owned property, and the quality and price of the dwellings. Rents should be set according to local demand and market conditions rather than central regulation, and landlords should have the power to react to changes in demand. So if landlords could not let their properties they should have the flexibility to reduce rents to the level that matches demand, let the properties to other groups such as students, or, as a last resort, demolish them. This is what municipal landlords in the Netherlands are

Box 3 **Ending social housing**
- a common legal standing for all landlords
- a common tenancy for rented housing
- compulsory stock transfer
- local planning framework
- abolition of Regional Boards and the Housing Corporation

able to do, and we should see it merely as the logical extension of a choice-based system. If we want people to be able to make choices we should also be prepared to deal with the consequences of those choices. If those choices communicate the fact that some housing is unpopular we then have a direct signal and landlords should be able to respond. This is in contrast to the current housing market renewal pathfinders, which have a prescribed target for demolitions regardless of local opinion or the actual state of the housing stock.

Subsidies to households, not landlords

Proper choice can be achieved through the privatisation of housing so that there is no distinction between landlords except in terms of quality, price and the location and type of their properties. But this is only half of what is necessary. In addition to changing the nature of landlords, we also need to change the manner in which housing is subsidised. There would be little point in reforming tenure without also making changes to subsidies (see Box 4).

The way to achieve this is by the reform of housing benefit to create a flat-rate housing allowance. A flat-rate local housing

Box 4 **Changing subsidies**
- abolition of supply-side subsidies
- only subsidy to be a flat-rate local housing allowance paid directly to households
- tight definition of vulnerability to include only those not capable of looking after themselves

allowance should be paid to households on the basis of their circumstances. The current housing benefit reforms, as discussed in Chapter 5, involve the introduction of a standard housing allowance and direct payments to tenants instead of making payments to their landlord. These go some way to achieving this general principle. The government's proposals, however, are currently intended only for the private rented sector, with nothing more than a non-specific aspiration to extend it to the social sector some time after 2012. Indeed, the Welfare Reform Green Paper (DWP, 2006) appears to be stepping away from extending these reforms to the social sector.

This housing allowance should be used to replace all other forms of subsidy, including capital subsidies paid to landlords. The aim of subsidy should be to ensure that households are able to exercise some choice over their housing. In part this can be achieved by encouraging competition between landlords, but tenants also need to be able to make an effective choice. Concentrating only on income-based subsidies means that these can be more generous than at present to allow low-income households a wider choice and give landlords proper incentives to let their houses to them. With total social housing expenditure in

2005/06 of over £7 billion, it would be possible to have a 50 per cent increase in housing benefit costs without any total increase in government housing-related expenditure (Wilcox, 2005).

The first reform, therefore, should be the ending of supply-side subsidies. This would allow for additional funds for a reformed housing benefit system offering a flat-rate allowance of 105 per cent of middle-market average rents for the locality. This allowance, as is the case with the current government's housing benefit reforms, would be based on the existing system of local reference rents. This system sets rents at the middle of the market for particular property types for each local authority area. The only distinctions in property types that I wish to maintain, however, are between single-person, couples' and family housing. As with current income support regulations, no distinction should be made for family size.

This more generous allowance would allow for proper incentives as well as encouraging landlords in the private sector to continue to let to housing benefit recipients. One of the consequences of the restrictions to housing benefit since 1996 has been a reluctance among private landlords to accept housing benefit claimants as tenants. Wilcox (1999) suggests that as a result the private rented sector started to decline for the first time since the deregulation of the sector in 1989. He attributes this decline to 'the restrictions on private rents eligible for housing benefit introduced at the beginning of 1996' (ibid.: 72). Between May 1997 and May 1998 there was a reduction of 100,000 private tenants claiming housing benefit, 'and most of that fall can be attributed to the benefit restrictions' (ibid.: 72). In 1996 46.6 per cent of private tenants were in receipt of housing benefit compared with only 28.7 per cent in 2003 (Wilcox, 2005). One might suggest that this shows that private landlords have not taken kindly to changes in housing benefit. But it also demonstrates that the private rented sector reacts quite quickly to changes in incentives. One might argue, then, that once there is a common tenancy and a more generous benefit system – so that there is effectively nothing but private landlords – landlords would have less resistance to housing benefit. What the response of private landlords to housing benefit changes shows is that the sector is responsive and sensitive to changes in market signals. In addition, the effect of a common tenancy for all landlords regardless of their history would create competition and lead to different stratifications and segmentation in the housing market to the benefit of households seeking different types of housing at widely differing costs.

An important principle of a flat-rate system should be that it is neutral in terms of household composition and characteristics: flat rate should mean nothing more than that a given amount is paid to a household. So there should be no premiums for particular types of household, and nor should there be reductions merely because a claimant is under 25, as is currently the case. Eligibility for benefit should be on the basis of income and should not encourage any particular lifestyle choices, just as mortgage repayments or salaries do not vary because of the composition of the household. As I discuss below, we should seek a housing system that is based on the proper contractual relationship between landord and tenant, and which is not complicated by the idea that some households have a 'special' need deserving of differential treatment from the landlord.

As I have suggested above, the only moderation to this principle is with regard to household size. The local housing allowance should be flexible enough to distinguish between single people, couples (living as a household) and families with children. This flexibility is needed to deal with the legitimate difference in rents between large and small dwellings and to deal with the potential problems of up-marketing and under-occupation. This simple banding of the local housing allowance will also help prevent collusion between landlord and tenant.

This raises the whole issue of what incentives are created by this new system of housing allowances. It might be argued, for instance, that this system might encourage households to fragment and live separately to increase their total income.[1] But the current benefit system has these incentives within it already, and indeed in a rather more severe way, in that lone parents receive an additional premium. The system proposed here, therefore, will provide less of an incentive than the current system.

But perhaps the most effective way of dealing with this problem is to see it not as a matter of system design but one of fraud. If a system operates under clear and publicly available regulations there is no excuse for abuse and action should be taken accordingly. We should not stall on reform because a system might carry with it some unwanted incentives, especially when we are capable of identifying what these incentives are in advance and taking measures against the resulting practices if and when they occur.

One group that will be better off under these proposals is young single people, in that the single-room rent regulation, restricting benefit to the cost of shared accommodation, will be

---

1   Perhaps the most problematic situation is where this happens fraudulently. For example, where the benefit is determined by household income and there is only one earner in a household, the earner has an incentive to declare that he or she lives at a separate address (for example, his or her parents' address) while actually living at the address of the claimant.

abolished. The restrictions in the allowance would not, however, allow them to under-occupy a property, and thus benefit disproportionately. The important principle here is that we should not make arbitrary judgements about claimants, as is the case with the single-room rent regulation.

Under the current housing benefit system, benefit is withdrawn using a 65 per cent taper. This means that for every £1 earned above the income support level 65 pence of benefit is withdrawn. Many critics have argued that this taper, combined with the tax and National Insurance system, which kicks in at a very low level of income, acts as a considerable disincentive to take up employment. This is because a claimant coming off benefit needs to earn considerably above the income support level to be any better off than if remaining on benefit. As Garnett and Perry (2005) have argued, however, merely making the tapers less steep would not have a great effect on work incentives. They argue that a more viable alternative would be the incorporation of housing benefit into the system of tax credits. This takes the discussion beyond the scope of this paper, but Garnett and Perry do make the point that a flat-rate housing allowance makes it easier to incorporate housing costs in a system of tax credits, as it eases out a lot of variation in eligible costs.

Therefore I would argue for maintaining the housing benefit taper at its current position for the moment. A government serious about reforming housing subsidies, however, must also look at the structures of social security benefits more generally, and in particular how they might be integrated with the tax system. The proposals discussed here would make a significant contribution to a more rational system of housing support for households on low income. But it should be seen as only part of a package. Indeed, the logical conclusion of the principle of neutrality considered here is to move away from specific housing supports altogether and instead incorporate a notional allowance for housing costs into a reformed system of income maintenance. This, though, is a much more long-term project, which need not get in the way of the necessary reforms presented in this paper.

The basis of any housing subsidy system should be to assume that individuals are competent and capable. Instead of the apparent assumption that all social housing tenants are vulnerable or have 'complex needs', we should assume that households can control their income and make decisions for themselves. We can make provision for those individuals who clearly cannot, but we should see these households as the exceptions and not as typical of the sector (King and Oxley, 2000). We currently have a housing system that assumes that households are not competent and capable if their income falls below a certain level and they are thus eligible for social housing. Once their income exceeds this level, however, they are deemed to be capable of managing their own affairs in the housing market. If one is a social housing tenant it is deemed that one needs housing professionals, working in local authorities and housing associations, to create policies and strategies to ensure that one's needs are met. One is deemed to be in need of support and so there is a whole structure in place, backed by centralised standards and targets, to ensure that one is no longer vulnerable. Increasingly, this has involved the punitive use of anti-social behaviour legislation to ensure that others, as well as yourself, behave as you should. If one is not a social housing tenant, however, it is assumed that one does not need these structures and can make proper decisions for oneself. Competence is therefore apparently a matter of housing tenure.

Of course, this is an absurdity, and one should assume that all individuals are equally capable of taking decisions and dealing with the consequences. This, then, should be the basis of any housing system, which should rest on the principle of minimising distinctions between households and their access to housing. There should be a neutrality on the part of government in which the only criteria for support is the income of a household. We can readily point to those who are not capable and devise individualised strategies to deal with them. In moving to this form of housing supports the UK will only be moving in the same direction as Australia, New Zealand and the USA, as well as other European countries such as the Netherlands.

In terms of abolishing supply-side subsidies and implementing the new flat-rate system, it is important for government to be clear and strong in dealing with the various interests. The way to manage this is to set a clear timetable for the implementation, whereby government announces a firm date for ending supports to landlords and for the introduction of a reformed housing benefit system. This timetable should be reasonably short – say, no more than three years – and be adhered to strictly. It would greatly assist this process if the government made no other reforms in this period. What reforms of this nature require is certainty and an implacable resolve on the part of government in dealing with the inevitable opposition and lobbying that will come from vested interests and political opponents.

We should not expect the process of reform to be straightforward and trouble-free. Indeed, the reform of housing allowances in the UK is particularly complicated and fraught with difficulties. This can be used as an excuse not to change things, but rather what is needed is government to adhere to a set of principles and implement them tenaciously, even in the face of opposition and conflict. If these principles are correct they should be adhered to. Of course, some individuals will be worse off while others benefit, but this is in the very nature of change. Moreover, the very purpose of the change is to make a difference to individuals.

What is incumbent on a government implementing these reforms is to explain, in a clear and precise manner, the purpose of the reforms and what benefits they will bring. It must also try to impress on all parties that the reforms will go ahead and will not be attenuated or moderated. This, of course, is a difficult point to get across, in that the recent history of government action does not encourage any sense of certainty or clarity. It is essential, however, for this sense to be given if the reforms are to be implemented with the minimum of disruption. Giving a clear timetable will allow for the affected parties to prepare for the changes, and this is why government should ensure that no other changes are pending during this period.

Many academics and commentators argue that without supply-side subsidies landlords will have no incentive to build new housing. The claim is that housing shortages cannot be remedied without some incentive to the supply side, and so government needs to provide subsidies to ensure that enough new housing is built. But this argument is based on the premise that if households are not able to afford to live where and in what dwellings they want, it is a problem for government to solve: in other words, it is assumed that, if people wish to live in a high-cost area, then they ought to be able to regardless of their income. Of course, the opportunity to live wherever one wants is something that might be desired, and I can certainly come up with a detailed demand for a pleasant cottage on the North Norfolk coast. The problem, however, is in thinking that one has a right to have one's request fulfilled, and that it needs to be fulfilled by government. Much of what is referred to as the 'housing crisis' arises from precisely this notion that we have the right to live where we want. Housing, or the need for shelter, is an imperative, but so are food and clothing, and we do not have a similar right to eat what we want and wear what we want, regardless of whether we can afford it. So we need to ask whether it is legitimate for us to base housing policy on what are maximal wants and desires in a manner that does not operate in other markets. Of course, there are peculiarities with housing, particularly its immobility. But many markets have structural imperfections which have to be lived with. What we should not do is use market imperfections as an excuse for government regulation, which will merely introduce many more of its own 'imperfections'.

But we also need to remember that altering the designation of housing from social to private does not alter the number of dwellings in circulation. One of the myths created by opponents of the Right to Buy was that it reduced the number of available dwellings. In fact it merely reduced the total stock of social dwellings. But even here none of those dwellings sold would necessarily have been available to let to the homeless if the Right to Buy had not existed: if these tenants liked their dwellings enough to purchase them, why assume they would leave them?

But despite the Right to Buy there are still over 5 million social dwellings in Great Britain (over 4 million in England alone), and so we can hardly claim that there is a lack of social housing. If we are to believe recent housing policy, the issue is not a shortage of rented housing, but a shortage of housing for owner occupation in certain parts of the country. Policy regarding social housing since

1997 has focused not on the scale of the sector, but on quality. As we saw in Chapter 5, resource accounting had the effect of institutionalising the landlord function of local authorities instead of their historic development role. Stock transfer, ALMOs and the PFI are aimed at injecting private finance into social housing to improve its quality, and this is backed up by the Decent Homes Standard. These policies are not aimed at increasing the size of the stock, but rather at maintaining the current stock to a high standard. Indeed, policies such as the housing market renewal pathfinders involve the demolition of a considerable amount of both private and public housing, often in the face of local opposition. More recently the Homes for All agenda appears to seek to shift resources away from social housing to low-cost ownership. So again, it would be difficult to claim that the problem is one of a shortage of social housing. This does not mean that new housing does not need to be built, but most of it is likely to be needed in the owner-occupied sector. Where new rented housing is needed this can be facilitated by a more consistent and generous system of housing allowances.

A new form of housing management

As I discussed in Chapter 5, the introduction of direct payments is likely to have a significant impact on the way landlords operate. While this can be mitigated in part at least by an increase in the levels of support, thereby not restricting landlord income, the biggest problem relates to the certainty of payment. This is not due to any inherent quality of tenants, but is rather the result of two generations of state dependency, which has meant that the majority of tenants do not feel responsible for their own rent payments. The government appears to believe that this 50-year period of inculcation can be altered merely by a change of policy, but this is unlikely to be the case. As American experiences have shown (Rogers, 1999), this sort of fundamental change in individualised benefits needs to be properly managed. This can be facilitated by offering a clear time-limited implementation plan backed up by wide publicity about the changes. As I have stated, this requires government to be implacable and certain in its strategy.

So what matters is the *form* of intervention that is required in this new privatised and tenure-neutral system. In order for this policy to work there is a need for the focus of housing to shift towards rent collection and arrears management. This is not intended to be punitive, but is rather a re-emphasising of the welfare function of housing. By this means we should seek to return to a more personalised form of intervention that seeks to help households manage their finances and learn to fulfil their responsibilities. This could be facilitated by a shift away from generalised housing management with its ever-extending role, where ever more policies, strategies and coordinating bodies are required. The priority for landlords and local welfare bodies should be to provide a system of support structures such as case workers and advisers to assist new and existing tenants in managing their finances and rent payments.

One would expect this change in priorities to occur as a result of self-interest as soon as housing benefit is paid directly to tenants. Government can offer a clear signal for change, however, by dismantling much of the regulation imposed on landlords, which serves to make landlords accountable upwards to government and not downwards to tenants. Governments like to talk about empowerment and concepts such as 'double devolution',

---

Box 5 A new housing management
- targets and performance to be set internally and not by any other body
- emphasis on basic management and maintenance, not strategy and 'community development'
- case-based housing management to support the individual decision-making of tenants

---

but this can only be achieved through a transfer of resources and not by central direction.

Finally, as should now be becoming clear, these reforms will fundamentally alter the way in which what were formerly social landlords operate (see Box 5). Instead of being concerned with strategic issues and community development, housing associations will have to reorient themselves towards their basic functions of ensuring that their properties are well managed, that rents are collected, that properties are allocated properly and fairly, and that tenancy regulations are enforced. These are the tasks in which landlords are expert and which they ought to be focusing on, rather than the more grandiose plans of the National Housing Federation and other bodies. Instead of having these basic tasks monitored by the current system of performance indicators, Best Value and inspections, we should rely on competition between landlords and the decision-making capabilities of individual households to pressurise them. This pressure from their customers will offer sufficient incentives to landlords and cure them of their apparent view that managing and maintaining housing are not enough. Landlords, instead of having to follow the whims of government, will now have to respond to their tenants' needs.

The immediate response one can expect from those wishing to protect the interests of social landlords is that tenants are vulnerable and not able to take care of their own interests. Indeed, there will always be some households that are genuinely vulnerable and will need high levels of support, and it is perfectly legitimate for these needs to be identified and met using government subsidy. But equally there is no reason why this support should not be located within the household rather than within any particular agency. What has become noticeable in recent years, however, is the extension of the categories of the vulnerable to include most social housing tenants. Indeed, for some commentators there is no distinction to be made between social housing tenants and the vulnerable. The problem with this perspective is that it soon becomes self-justifying, as can be seen in the case of current housing benefit reforms. If individuals are treated as incapable then it is likely that they will soon concur, and this is what has happened when housing benefit has been paid to landlords.

This means that any shift towards the structures I have proposed cannot be achieved overnight. As I have already suggested, there will be a need to shift resources towards arrears management and case work for the first few years of the new housing allowance system. This will ensure that landlords retain their financial viability and there is not a massive increase in evictions and homelessness. Housing is not the complex business it is often portrayed to be. It involves straightforward and regular tasks, most of which can be planned in advance and dealt with in a programmatical manner. Of course, we can turn any task into a complex one, and there may be some incentive on the part of the social housing profession to do so. But quite often one fears that this pleading about the difficulty of the problems facing them prevents professionals and the organisations they represent from getting on with what they ought to be doing.

8 CONCLUSION: LIBERATING LANDLORDS AND TENANTS

This paper has sought to criticise current housing policies and present the outline of an alternative structure for rented housing. The problems with current policy are as much cultural as structural, with many in housing concentrating on overblown and abstract ideals rather than the basic tasks of housing management and maintenance. They are, however, encouraged to do this by the current policy framework. The aim of these proposals is to develop genuine choice, so that this is not merely a tool with which to beat landlords and to force them to 'modernise', and policy empowers households so they can use their dwelling as they wish to.

The basis of any housing policy should be an understanding that housing is essentially a private activity based around the aims and interests of individual and separate households. Therefore it is these interests which should be paramount in any system of housing provision. For the most part a market can assist in ensuring that households fulfil their interests, but for some people additional support will be needed. This does not mean, however, that we ignore the fundamental point that all households should make decisions for themselves and be accountable for those decisions.

The key to achieving this is competition, and this involves the reform of tenancy law and subsidy systems to ensure that there are no distinctions between landlords: all landlords should be private, regardless of whom they house and the manner in which they choose to orient themselves. The more landlords that can be encouraged to enter the market, the more tenants will benefit and the more choice they will have. Crucial to this process is a policy to move subsidies to the demand side in the form of more generous housing allowances. These should be tenure-neutral and aim to attain the maximum neutrality between landlords. The ability to pay rent should be the sole criterion for access. Supply-side subsidies would cease, thus ensuring that no overall increase in the housing budget would be necessary.

These policies are genuinely aimed at putting people first. The government seeks to do this with its *Sustainable Communities* plan, but as we have seen, the main beneficiary of current housing policies is the Treasury. I have shown that it is quite false to argue that services can be centralised *and* personalised at the same time. The centralisation of housing policy is the real problem that needs tackling. If it is not, the notion of choice will soon become a discredited term, being too closely associated with policies that are aimed at achieving precisely the opposite of individual choice.

But the key point is that choice and social housing do not mix. The types of choice currently on offer to social housing applicants and tenants are not real, but rather are mere attempts to control social landlords under the illusion of empowerment. But genuine empowerment means government letting go of power and not seeking to determine outcomes for people. So if we want proper choice, whereby people can make decisions and are accountable for them, then we cannot retain social housing. But if we want to keep control at the centre and allow government to manage housing, if we want to determine the rents landlords can charge and how they spend their money, and if we want government to dictate how and whom they house, then we should not purport to be promoting choice. In these latter conditions choice is an illusion: it is simply not possible to have proper choices in the hemmed-in and constrained world created by the government. In this paper I have made a clear case in favour of choice, and accordingly I have stated, and sought to justify, that there is therefore no future for social housing.

REFERENCES

Albon, R. and D. Stafford (1987), *Rent Control*, London: Croom Helm.

Audit Commission (2005), *Financing Council Housing*, London: Audit Commission.

Boddie, M. (1992), 'From mutual interests to market forces', in C. Grant (ed.), *Built to Last? Reflections on British Housing Policy*, London: Roof.

Borrie Commission (1995), *Social Justice: Strategies for National Renewal*, London: Vintage Press.

Boyne, G. et al. (2003), *Evaluating Public Management Reforms*, Buckingham: Open University Press.

Bramley, G. and H. Pawson (2002), 'Low demand for housing: extent, incidence and national policy implications', *Urban Studies*, 39(3): 393–422.

Brown, T. (ed.) (1999), *Stakeholder Housing: A Third Way*, London: Pluto Press.

Brown, T. and P. King (2005), 'The power to choose: effective choice and housing policy', *European Journal of Housing Policy*, 5(1): 59–75.

Brown, T. and J. Passmore (1998), *Housing and Anti-Poverty Strategies: A Good Practice Guide*, York: Joseph Rowntree Foundation/Chartered Institute of Housing.

Brown, T., A. Dearling, R. Hunt, J. Richardson and N. Yates (2002), *Allocate or Let – Your Choice*, Coventry and York: Chartered Institute of Housing/Joseph Rowntree Foundation.

Burrows, R. (2003), 'How the other half lives? An exploratory analysis of poverty and home ownership in Britain', *Urban Studies*, 40(7): 1223–42.

Clapham, D. (2005), *The Meaning of Housing: A Pathways Approach*, Bristol: Policy Press.

DETR (Department of the Environment, Transport and the Regions) (2000), *Quality and Choice: A Decent Home for All*, London: DETR/DSS.

Devigne, R. (1994), *Recasting Conservatism: Oakeshott, Strauss, and the Response to Postmodernism*, New Haven, CT: Yale University Press.

DOE (Department of the Environment) (1987), *Housing: The Government's Proposals*, London: HMSO.

DWP (Department for Work and Pensions) (2002), *Building Choice and Responsibility: A Radical Agenda for Housing Benefit*, London: Department for Work and Pensions.

DWP (2006), *A New Deal for Welfare: Empowering People to Work*, London: Department for Work and Pensions.

Garnett, D. and J. Perry (2005), *Housing Finance*, Coventry: Chartered Institute of Housing.

HM Treasury (2004), *Review of Housing Supply: Securing our Future Housing Needs*, London: HMSO (also known as the Barker Report).

Jenkins, S. (1995), *Accountable to None: The Tory Nationalisation of Britain*, London: Hamish Hamilton.

Kemp, P. (1997), *A Comparative Study of Housing Allowances*, London: HMSO.

King, P. (1996), *The Limits of Housing Policy: A Philosophical Investigation*, London: Middlesex University Press.

King, P. (1998), *Housing, Individuals and the State: The Morality of Government Intervention*, London: Routledge.

King, P. (1999), 'The reform of housing benefit', *Economic Affairs*, 19(3): 9–13.

King, P. (2000), *Housing Benefit: What Government Ought to Do, but Won't*, London: Adam Smith Institute.

King, P. (2001), *Understanding Housing Finance*, London: Routledge.

King, P. (2003), *A Social Philosophy of Housing*, Aldershot: Ashgate.

King, P. (2004), *Private Dwelling: Contemplating the Use of Housing*, Abingdon: Routledge.

King, P. (2006), *A Conservative Consensus?: Housing Policy Before 1997 and After*, Exeter: Imprint Academic.

King, P. and M. Oxley (2000), *Housing: Who Decides?*, Basingstoke: Macmillan.

Malpass, P. and H. Aughton (1999), *Housing Finance: A Basic Guide*, 5th edn, London: Shelter.

Malpass, P. and A. Murie (1999), *Housing Policy and Practice*, 5th edn, Basingstoke: Macmillan.

Marsh, A. et al. (2004), *Piloting Choice-based Lettings: An Evaluation*, London: ODPM.

Marsland, D. (1996), *Welfare or Welfare State? Contradictions and Dilemmas in Social Policy*, Basingstoke: Macmillan.

NHF (National Housing Federation) (2003), 'iN business for communities: action for change', London: NHF.

ODPM (Office of the Deputy Prime Minister) (2003), *Sustainable Communities: Building for the Future*, London: ODPM.

ODPM (2005a), *Sustainable Communities: Homes for All: A Five Year Plan from the ODPM*, London: ODPM.

ODPM (2005b), *Planning for Housing Provision*, London: ODPM.

Oxley, M. and J. Smith (1996), *Housing Policy and Rented Housing in Europe*, London: Spon.

Page, D. (1993), *Building for Communities*, York: Joseph Rowntree Foundation.

Pawson, H. (2004), 'Reviewing stock transfer', in S. Wilcox (ed.), *UK Housing Review, 2004/2005*, pp. 11–19.

Power, A. (1987), *Property before People: The Management of Twentieth Century Council Housing*, Hemel Hempstead: Allen & Unwin.

Power, A. (1993), *From Hovels to Highrise: State Housing in Europe since 1850*, London: Routledge.

Pratchett, L. (2002), 'Local government: from modernisation to consolidation', *Parliamentary Affairs*, 55: 331–46.

Rogers, J. (1999), 'Getting Wisconsin to work', *Economic Affairs*, 19(3): 28–34.

Turner, J. F. C. (1976), *Housing by People: Towards Autonomy in Building Environments*, London: Marion Boyars.

Wilcox, S. (1999), *Housing Finance Review, 1999/2000*, York: Joseph Rowntree Foundation.

Wilcox, S. (ed.) (2005), *UK Housing Review, 2005/2006*, Coventry: Chartered Institute of Housing/Council for Mortgage Lenders.

ABOUT THE IEA

The Institute is a research and educational charity (No. CC 235 351), limited by guarantee. Its mission is to improve understanding of the fundamental institutions of a free society by analysing and expounding the role of markets in solving economic and social problems.

The IEA achieves its mission by:

- a high-quality publishing programme
- conferences, seminars, lectures and other events
- outreach to school and college students
- brokering media introductions and appearances

The IEA, which was established in 1955 by the late Sir Antony Fisher, is an educational charity, not a political organisation. It is independent of any political party or group and does not carry on activities intended to affect support for any political party or candidate in any election or referendum, or at any other time. It is financed by sales of publications, conference fees and voluntary donations.

In addition to its main series of publications the IEA also publishes a termly journal, *Economic Affairs*.

The IEA is aided in its work by a distinguished international Academic Advisory Council and an eminent panel of Honorary Fellows. Together with other academics, they review prospective IEA publications, their comments being passed on anonymously to authors. All IEA papers are therefore subject to the same rigorous independent refereeing process as used by leading academic journals.

IEA publications enjoy widespread classroom use and course adoptions in schools and universities. They are also sold throughout the world and often translated/reprinted.

Since 1974 the IEA has helped to create a worldwide network of 100 similar institutions in over 70 countries. They are all independent but share the IEA's mission.

Views expressed in the IEA's publications are those of the authors, not those of the Institute (which has no corporate view), its Managing Trustees, Academic Advisory Council members or senior staff.

Members of the Institute's Academic Advisory Council, Honorary Fellows, Trustees and Staff are listed on the following page.

The Institute gratefully acknowledges financial support for its publications programme and other work from a generous benefaction by the late Alec and Beryl Warren.

The Institute of Economic Affairs
2 Lord North Street, Westminster, London SW1P 3LB
Tel: 020 7799 8900
Fax: 020 7799 2137
Email: iea@iea.org.uk
Internet: iea.org.uk

Director General & Ralph Harris Fellow Mark Littlewood

Editorial Director   Professor Philip Booth

Managing Trustees

Chairman: Professor D R Myddelton
Kevin Bell   Professor Mark Pennington
Robert Boyd   Neil Record
Michael Fisher   Professor Martin Ricketts
Michael Hintze   Linda Whetstone
Professor Patrick Minford

Academic Advisory Council

Chairman: Professor Martin Ricketts
Graham Bannock   Dr Eileen Marshall
Dr Roger Bate   Professor Antonio Martino
Professor Alberto Benegas-Lynch, Jr Dr John Meadowcroft
Professor Donald J Boudreaux   Dr Anja Merz
Professor John Burton   Professor Julian Morris
Professor Forrest Capie   Professor Alan Morrison
Professor Steven N S Cheung   Paul Ormerod
Professor Tim Congdon   Professor David Parker
Professor N F R Crafts   Professor Victoria Curzon Price
Professor David de Meza   Professor Colin Robinson
Professor Kevin Dowd   Professor Charles K Rowley
Professor Richard A Epstein   Professor Pascal Salin
Nigel Essex   Dr Razeen Sally
Professor David Greenaway   Professor Pedro Schwartz
Dr Ingrid A Gregg   Professor J R Shackleton
Walter E Grinder   Jane S Shaw
Professor Steve H Hanke   Professor W Stanley Siebert
Professor Keith Hartley   Dr Elaine Sternberg
Professor David Henderson   Professor James Tooley
Professor Peter M Jackson   Professor Nicola Tynan
Dr Jerry Jordan   Professor Roland Vaubel
Dr Lynne Kiesling   Dr Cento Veljanovski
Professor Daniel B Klein   Professor Lawrence H White
Professor Chandran Kukathas   Professor Walter E Williams
Dr Tim Leunig   Professor Geoffrey E Wood
Professor Stephen C Littlechild

Honorary Fellows

Professor Armen A Alchian   Professor Chiaki Nishiyama
Professor Michael Beenstock   Professor Sir Alan Peacock
Sir Samuel Brittan   Professor Anna J Schwartz
Professor James M Buchanan   Professor Vernon L Smith
Professor Ronald H Coase   Professor Gordon Tullock
Professor David Laidler   Professor Basil S Yamey

Other papers recently published by the IEA include:

Taxation and Red Tape
The Cost to British Business of Complying with the UK Tax System
Francis Chittenden, Hilary Foster & Brian Sloan
Research Monograph 64; ISBN 978 0 255 36612 0; £12.50

Ludwig von Mises – A Primer
Eamonn Butler
Occasional Paper 143; ISBN 978 0 255 36629 8; £7.50

Does Britain Need a Financial Regulator?
Statutory Regulation, Private Regulation and Financial Markets
Terry Arthur & Philip Booth
Hobart Paper 169; ISBN 978 0 255 36593 2; £12.50

Hayek's *The Constitution of Liberty*
An Account of Its Argument
Eugene F. Miller
Occasional Paper 144; ISBN 978 0 255 36637 3; £12.50

Fair Trade Without the Froth
A Dispassionate Economic Analysis of 'Fair Trade'
Sushil Mohan
Hobart Paper 170; ISBN 978 0 255 36645 8; £10.00

A New Understanding of Poverty
Poverty Measurement and Policy Implications
Kristian Niemietz
Research Monograph 65; ISBN 978 0 255 36638 0; £12.50

The Challenge of Immigration
A Radical Solution
Gary S. Becker
Occasional Paper 145; ISBN 978 0 255 36613 7; £7.50

Sharper Axes, Lower Taxes
Big Steps to a Smaller State
Edited by Philip Booth
Hobart Paperback 38; ISBN 978 0 255 36648 9; £12.50

Self-employment, Small Firms and Enterprise
Peter Urwin
Research Monograph 66; ISBN 978 0 255 36610 6; £12.50

Crises of Governments
The Ongoing Global Financial Crisis and Recession
Robert Barro
Occasional Paper 146; ISBN 978 0 255 36657 1; £7.50

... and the Pursuit of Happiness
Wellbeing and the Role of Government
Edited by Philip Booth
Readings 64; ISBN 978 0 255 36656 4; £12.50

Public Choice – A Primer
Eamonn Butler
Occasional Paper 147; ISBN 978 0 255 36650 2; £10.00

Other IEA publications

Comprehensive information on other publications and the wider work of the IEA can be found at www.iea.org.uk. To order any publication please see below.

Personal customers

Orders from personal customers should be directed to the IEA:
Clare Rusbridge
IEA
2 Lord North Street
FREEPOST LON10168
London SW1P 3YZ
Tel: 020 7799 8907. Fax: 020 7799 2137
Email: crusbridge@iea.org.uk

Trade customers

All orders from the book trade should be directed to the IEA's distributor:
Gazelle Book Services Ltd (IEA Orders)
FREEPOST RLYS-EAHU-YSCZ
White Cross Mills
Hightown
Lancaster LA1 4XS
Tel: 01524 68765. Fax: 01524 53232
Email: sales@gazellebooks.co.uk

IEA subscriptions

The IEA also offers a subscription service to its publications. For a single annual payment (currently £42.00 in the UK), subscribers receive every monograph the IEA publishes. For more information please contact:
Clare Rusbridge
Subscriptions
IEA
2 Lord North Street
FREEPOST LON10168
London SW1P 3YZ
Tel: 020 7799 8907. Fax: 020 7799 2137
Email: crusbridge@iea.org.uk